FORGIVE *for* YOU

A MEMOIR OF FAMILY, FURY, AND FREEDOM

LUCA OAKE

Forgive For You: A Memoir of Family, Fury, and Freedom

Published by One of Hearts Press
An imprint of Hearts of Gold Creative LLC

Paperback ISBN 979-8-9865873-4-9
Ebook ISBN: 979-8-9865873-5-6
Audiobook ISBN: 979-8-9865873-6-3
Hardcover ISBN: 979-8-9865873-7-0

Explore forgiveness at youforgiveforyou.community
Connect with Luca Oake at hello@youforgiveforyou.community
Connect with Hearts of Gold at heartsofgoldcreative.com

Dear Readers

You'll likely notice the first-person i is lowercased throughout this book. It's not a typo.

For years, i've been decapitalizing the i when writing personally. It started with texting and eventually showed up in journaling, in emails, and on social media. It's a constant battle with auto-correct, but i'm committed to there being no good-enough reason why my i is bigger than you, we, they, and us.

Millennials and other native thumb-communicators may not find a decapitalized i all that odd, but i've certainly been called out by writers, academics, and old-schoolers who find it off-putting and brain-glitching.

Everyday English abounds with word uses that were once flagrant fouls against word rules. Like how "literally" now also means the exact opposite of its original definition.

Or how it used to be grammatically wrong to say "We have over 30 years' experience" in this or that. According to The Associated Press Stylebook from 30 years ago, no you didn't because "over" is a preposition of physical position, and "years" is a countable noun. At some point, AP conceded to common usage, and now you can literally have "over" as many years as you want.

Since we can clearly change the rules, i'm going my own way when it comes to the size of letters in words. Where i do capitalize, my proper nouns are statements about the importance, respect or impact i'm assigning to people, objects, and ideas through words. Where i don't capitalize, it's because lowercase better represents my values.

Hence, my i will be uncapitalized, unless it appears in quoted speech.

Comparing grammar gripes is a favorite pastime of mine, and i wholly expect to run up against someone's grammar pet peeves with my unconventional capitalization and my idiosyncratic i.

In case this is you, i just wanted to say, i see you, and by the end of this book, i trust that you'll forgive me.

- Luca

Preface

Forgive For You exists as a book because the Universe harassed me to write it.

Like an unwanted houseguest, the idea for this book showed up from outta nowhere, parked itself in my life, and refused to be run off by the demanding practicalities of full-time work and student loan debt. When i insisted there's no way i had time to sit and write a book, i lost my job and found myself with all the time in the world. When i insisted there's no way i had money to launch a book, resources materialized to fund it.

For 3 years, i kept saying no to the idea, and it kept persisting. If that's not harassment, fine then, you tell me what to call it, i'm open-minded.

Life was once organized around my passions, what i wanted to do. Now, it's driven by this purpose, what i feel a need to do. While i have no idea who – if anyone – needs to read this book, for reasons i still don't get, i apparently needed to write it. So here it is.

For 30+ years, forgiveness has been changing my heart and mind for the better. This tool came into my life in my mid-20s, kickstarting what's become a reliable life practice. But that didn't seem to me like much to write about, especially not an entire book. All the sermons preached and ink spilled on forgiveness for more than 2,000 years, what more could my yammering add to the topic? The answer to that is, perhaps, not much.

And yet, with all that's been said about forgiveness, i've also wondered, why aren't we doing more of it? So often, i encounter people consciously and unconsciously gripped by resentment or resignation. We're so mad, it's killing us, and we don't know it. Or we give up and opt to suffer, with others, and with ourselves.

If we could forgive, we could be free of it. But we just won't let go.

Aside from watching movies and eating chocolate, the one thing i know i'm good at is turning terribly difficult experiences into evolutionary journeys, transforming trauma and pain into healing and growth through forgiveness.

So, goaded by unseen forces, i sat down, pounded on my keyboard, and produced this memoir with a message, *Forgive For You*. Exhausted by how we treat each other, exasperated at how we treat ourselves, this is what i'm offering to make a difference.

As i've worked through mess, missteps, and mending in my life, asking questions is how i've learned. My learning is shared here not because i'm endowed with abundant expertise, but because i do have a particular experience of living through hard things and finding a way to something softer.

Smart people learn from their own lives. Wise people learn from the lives of others. Maybe this is a wisdom opportunity to scoop up some gems and take them with you.

If you're carrying bitterness, grief, pain, or anything heavy, this book offers a way to lay it down without giving in. It's here to show you how healing can be a power move, and how forgiveness doesn't mean selling yourself short. It means setting yourself free.

Following each chapter is a landing zone of questions that invite you to pause, reflect, inhale, exhale, and integrate. If you're holding or hearing this book, it's no longer mine, it is now yours to do with as you see fit. Don't wanna do questions? Skip 'em. Don't wanna do them alone? Take 'em to your therapist, a friend, a mentor, your book group.

Don't do anything from this book that doesn't feel right for you. And definitely do what feels uncomfortable. That's when you're on your evolution-edge. That's how you grow.

As you read or listen, know that i'm curious about how this hits you – what you think, what you feel, what comes alive for you. If you wanna talk it through, i'm here. Reach out, share what's up with you and forgiveness. Say hello@youforgiveforyou.community.

- Luca

26 June 2025 Photo by Alora Daunt
Writing @ The Pearl Works, Monterey, California

WHAT'S INSIDE

0. UNFORGIVABLES

This book is about me, but i made it for you.

Who am i? Call me an ordinary person who's had an extraordinary collection of losses to survive and grievances to overcome.

Childhood innocence was lost to me by age 8. In adulthood, i lost my Parents and the foundational sense of safety we'd built together. Fewer than 5 years before writing this book, i lost a 10-year relationship and a marriage that i loved and thought would last till the end of time. Human hurt has tested and taxed my heart. Forgiveness helped heal it.

Who are you? Likely someone who's come here feeling somebody out there cannot or should not be forgiven. To that, i say welcome, Friend! You're in the right place. These days, we humans are a hot mess, and i'm not here to dissuade you from the plain truth about how funked up the world is. In fact, i say let's kick off our moment together with a list of folks who in our present 21st Century times clearly don't deserve forgiveness:

Allow me to get us started:

- fascists, racists, terrorists
- the Powerful and the Privileged
- one or more of our Parents
- family members who've betrayed or abandoned us
- friends who've failed or ghosted us
- partners who cheated when they vowed to be faithful, or left when they vowed to stay
- that mother who killed her children
- that cult leader who killed a bunch of people
- that person we loved who killed themselves

- alcoholics who won't stop drinking
- addicts who won't stop using
- school shooters, killer cops, sexual predators, child abusers
- internet scammers who target the elderly (gah! you worthless #$%@&)
- Big Oil, Big Banks, Big Pharma
- that boss who made work life a living hell
- narcissists, and gaslighters
- liars, cheats, and thieves

Reading this on paper? There's an extra page at the end of this chapter for your Personal List of Unforgivables. Or grab your journal and name some names. As a bumper sticker once read: "If you're not in rage, you're not paying attention." This is your safe space to rage, so let's go there. Call the Unforgivables as you see 'em.

We all know how vile and violating people can be. We know how careless, thoughtless and clueless people can be. Some of us know vicariously as we watch the world spin madly on. Too many of us have survived extensive firsthand experiences.

Back in my first year of undergraduate studies at a Women's college, i took a course on self-defense that included 12 female-identified students. When the instructor asked the group by a show of hands who among us had experienced sexual violation of any kind either as a child or adult, 10 of 12 people raised their hands.

Because of that moment in that course, when i find myself in a group, i often wonder about individuals: "How has your heart been disappointed or broken by the world?"

Is human-perpetuated trauma endemic to the human experience? Do any of us get away with lives that aren't touched by it?

Isn't it astounding that in this modern day and age, the only predators we have as humans remain OTHER HUMANS? It's enough pain to make one's head explode.

OK but ifi'mbeinghonest, looking back over the suggested List of Unforgivables, i've been roughly 5 to 8 of those kinds of people. Sometimes, i genuinely had no idea that was me, but sometimes, i knew exactly who i was being and what i was doing, and there was no indication at the time that i had much propensity to do better or be better.

It took time, effort, commitment, support, and an assist from Good Fortune for me to come anywhere near being a warm, decent human being, and even now, i STILL have work to do. Catch me on a day when my heart feels sore and tender from loss, lack, or loneliness. You're likely to encounter me at my least personable and most irritable - like a porcupine, soft and vulnerable on the inside, but sharp and menacing on the outside.

Sidenote about porcupines. According to Wikipedia, a baby porcupine is a porcupette, and it's born covered in soft hair. But within just *a few days*, those soft hairs harden into sharp adult quills.

Apparently, porcupettes need to grow up quickly. Given how early i experienced the world's insanity, i'm feeling like i landed on a porcupine timeline.

When i consider my List of Unforgivables and the prickly hard-heartedness it includes, i also can't help but think of my inner porcupine and wonder: Who out there would make an Unforgivables list that includes me? If i insist on being unforgiving, should someone else be holding me as unforgivable? Would doing so create anything good for anyone?

/ .- -.-. -.-. . .--. - .- -. -.-. . /

For the longest time, like 10+ years, i refused to say the first line of the Serenity Prayer.

(If this reads like a random segue, stay with me, it's relevant.)

The Serenity prayer came into my life via 12-step self-work just after i turned 23. As a deeply troubled and wildly unmanaged young adult pestered by suicidal ideation, i fully embraced needing courage to change what i could alongside the wisdom to know the difference between what i could and couldn't change. But i remained staunchly and violently opposed to the prayer's starting place: Accept the things i could not change.

Worse than defeat, acceptance lived in me like a kind of gross and toxic collusion with the wrongness of the world. If i accepted what i couldn't change, wouldn't i give these failures license to persist? Nope. Absolutely not. For me, acceptance felt unacceptable.

My troubled relationship with acceptance finds kinship with folks who express similarly staunch opposition to the idea of forgiveness. If we forgive those who continue to hurt us or others, aren't we condoning their harmful behavior? Isn't that letting perpetrators get away with their crimes against humanity? Isn't that letting ourselves be victimized? For many of us, forgiveness feels like betrayal, violation, self-harm. It is unacceptable.

But wait, where did we get our preconceptions of large life notions like acceptance and forgiveness in the first place? All the energy i spent wrestling with my preconceptions, i didn't think to start by questioning whether my preconceptions actually originated with me, or whether i'd been running my life on questionably effective hand-me-down ideas. Nor did it occur to me that i could, and likely should, examine these hand-me-downs and decide whether to upgrade my ideas.

As i got on with rooting out some of my rage and rigidity, and gave myself permission to rethink emotional positions that felt so firm and so true, i eventually came across a simple and revelatory declaration about acceptance and forgiveness that changed me.

Perhaps you, too, have encountered this idea already, but just in case not, or if it's had a hard time sticking, i'll offer it here for good measure:

Acceptance is not approval. Forgiveness is not excusal.

We resist acceptance or refuse to extend forgiveness because we believe this giving in would extend undeserved pardon, which could potentially weaken, violate or harm us. Rather than question where we got these ideas and whether they're worth holding on to, we live with the belief that acceptance and forgiveness undermine our personhood.

They do not. Quite the opposite, they actually can release and empower us.

Acceptance is not approval. Forgiveness is not excusal.

When we forgive, we don't pardon or excuse. We accept and transform. This is where many of us need a full-on cognitive reset and a lot of repetition to overcome long-held and unhelpful definitions and fallacies we're holding about what forgiveness actually is.

By forgiving, we make things right for ourselves, we do right for ourselves. We clear ourselves of grievance. We concede to reality and find our flow through what is.

We don't need ourselves to be in good moral standing, nor do we need anyone to say they're sorry, they should've done better, they regret their actions, they want to make amends, or they care to make things right for us.

Forgiveness needs only our committed participation to turn human mayhem into magic. This is precisely why forgiveness is one of the most sane and powerful choices we can make for our own better-being. If have ourselves, then we already have what we need.

We can practice forgiveness as an action that has little to do with the world at large or any of the actors in it. We don't need other people to be involved. Whomever we're forgiving need not be alive, present, available, deserving, willing, or able to participate.

No one need know about our forgiving for forgiveness to work its magic for us.

When we finally don't need change from people who couldn't come through for us in the first place, people who may never be anyone other than who they've been, we can be free. We come to know we can overcome anything, and life is no longer as scary.

Rather than continuing to tie ourselves up and tire ourselves out from resisting what is, we take hold of a thing that's happened to us and reshape it into a thing that happens for us. We forgive to free ourselves. We forgive for us. You forgive for you.

Now, to the real question: Do we want to be free from what pains us?

Even if we find ourselves in situations we desperately want to change, change is scary. Who will we be without the pain that's always been? Fortunately for me, my choices as a young adult were limited to change or die. For the things i could not change, all the things that grieved and pained and shamed me, i had to figure out something i could do. Turns out, for me, that something was forgive, and doing so saved my life.

You've heard people talk of finding forgiveness in your heart? Nope, my heart was too broken at the start. Forgiveness couldn't live in my heart. It needed to live in my body where my experiences burned. It needed to live in my mind, where my stories shouted. For me, i couldn't forgive and forget; i needed to forgive because i couldn't forget.

Our emotional needs are not always our allies. They do not always represent the most developed or strongest parts of ourselves. In my early adulthood, my emotional needs centered on acknowledgment and retribution. What i wanted most was for the people who raised me to own what they'd done, and to pay for it.

What i got instead was guidance to forgive. That guidance led to action that became a practice that transformed my life. What started as a necessity grew into a choice that set me free from resentment and retribution, and set me up to err on the side of love.

If not for the parents who raised me, i may not have needed so much forgiveness, and if i hadn't learned forgiveness, i wouldn't have eventually gotten parents who loved me.

Forgiving the family that made me allowed me to make a family that cherished me.

Intentionally and unintentionally, people are awful to each other. While i've come to appreciate John Lennon imagining all the people sharing all the world and living as one, i continue to expect we will inevitably harm each other. Not because we're bad, just because we're human. It's what we do.

Forgiveness is fundamental to my life because when i can forgive, i give myself peace.

If you're comfortable mentally and emotionally where you are, congratulations! You may not need forgiveness to make your way through the world. Maybe pass this book along to someone else who's struggling.

For anyone who has even one person you're holding as unforgivable, i've got a story that can maybe help with that. And i'm here to walk alongside you as we see about setting you free.

Let's Go There

- *Who's on your Personal List of Unforgivables?*

- *What about you internally keeps these Unforgivables on your list? What keeps you unwilling or unable to forgive?*

- *Who has you on their Personal List of Unforgivables?*

- *What about them internally keeps you on their Unforgivables list? What do you think keeps them unwilling or unable to forgive you?*

1. LOVE HEROES

For a bunch of years now, i've lived within an easy day's drive of where my Parents are buried in California, but i don't go visit their graves.

In proper fashion, we held moving memorials for both. First, for my Beloved Momma who died in May 2020, not of COVID, but of being a little old Black Lady from Alabama who spent way too many of her 78 years beset by hard work and poor health, and who anyways constantly put more emphasis on caring for others at the expense of herself.

By her 40s she'd lost 12 front teeth to rot – incisor to incisor, top and bottom. Raised in a 6-children farming family of meager means, she didn't grow up with good dental care and hadn't learned to think about protecting teeth she might want to keep for later. She left the South at 21 for opportunity in the West but found more strife than success.

She survived domestic violence and left an oppressive marriage to pour her life energy into caring for a daughter who died at 30, beleaguered by childhood-onset diabetes and substance abuse as an adult. She relocated her own ailing mother from Alabama to live with her full-time until her mother died. Still, from all her caretaking, my Beloved Momma gleaned little in the way of learning to care for herself.

No matter the cost, her existence revolved around the care of others. She comforted folks with flour, butter and sugar, baking for doctors and nurses who looked after her and my Dad. She gave wayward relatives what she could financially as she fretted over paying the bills. You couldn't run a quick errand with her in tow. She stopped to have a hug and a word with anyone for any reason or for no reason at all. She helped people feel seen, safe and supported. She inspired people to feel loved.

So many friends and neighbors and church folks saw her as a mother figure and called her Mom. As my Parents' only legal child, i felt compelled to stake my Only Child claim and address her as no one else did. That's how she came to be my Beloved Momma.

In me she had a care advocate, and my involvement extended and added peace to her life. Her stubborn independence and aversion to accepting help kept me from saving it.

Weakened in October 2019 by surgery to remove a cancerous kidney, and refusing all good-sense measures such as in-home care or using a cane, she fell while home alone during the 30 minutes my Dad had run out to pick up a prescription.

He'd sat her in her preferred armchair and implored her to stay put. She fractured her back after getting up to answer the doorbell. It proved to be the beginning of her end.

Because of COVID, we gathered in masks soaked in tears to watch from a distance as cemetery workers lowered her mahogany-colored casket into the ground. This section of the cemetery had just opened that Spring, and the air smelled of blooming flowers and wet earth from water sprayed over the dirt to keep the dust down. Everyone kept close and solemn with arms wrapped around shoulders, singing a bit, but i had to stay in the car because i couldn't stop scream-weeping as the earth welcomed her home.

My Dad, an Alabama native son who survived the American South's Emmett Till-era of brutal racism and two tours of infantry combat in Vietnam, died an Old Soldier in 2022. That he made it to 80 was a feat of sorts with his 4 comorbidities - COPD, diabetes, heart disease, and lymphocytic lymphoma. Any one of these is supposed to kill you.

But 5 days before he died, my Dad had the wherewithal to get himself outta bed and get into his typical outfit of pressed jeans held up by suspenders, a collared shirt, and one of his many Army baseball caps. He got himself into the kitchen to fix his favorite snack, a microwaved ham + cheese croissant sandwich with a side of doughnut balls, then got himself into his living room chair to watch his favorite show, WWE wrestling.

You wouldn't have known it to look at him, but that was his final meal.

Pops was a fighter forged from the sturdy stuff of the Silent Generation. He earned a Purple Heart for his Vietnam combat wounds and a Bronze Star for valor and talked very rarely and never in detail about what he did during the war to merit these medals.

Because the Universe timed my Dad's passing perfectly at the start of November, we memorialized him on Veterans Day befitting his military legacy. American flags flanked his open casket. His memorial service included a join-if-the-spirit-moved-you march up and down the chapel's aisles to gospel songs.

We buried him the day before Thanksgiving with a funeral procession led by veteran Patriot Guard Riders on motorcycles, followed by the military honors of a flag-folding ceremony and a rifle salute, the one thing he'd told me he wanted.

An only child's life can be a lonesome thing, but it can also be incredibly liberating. As the one person vested with decision-making authority, i could steward their end-of-life journey with spacious ease and little drama. My aims were to bring family - given and chosen - into an experience as joyful and love-filled as my Parents' lives had been.

Obituaries, casket details, music, photo slideshows, a litany of pastors and speakers, all the particulars that went into planning their goodbyes i realize now helped transition me into the rest of my life without them. It's a privilege to have a cemetery marker that says they were here. But i don't go there because for me, it's not really where they are.

/ .-.. --- ...- . /

The loving version of my Parents came into my life as i entered my late 20s. For our first family outing, they introduced me to Las Vegas. They lived a couple hours' drive away in a desert town with dry heat to mitigate the rheumatoid arthritis my Beloved Momma picked up while laboring in the damp cold of naval shipyards. Her ailing joints didn't hinder her slot machine playing abilities, though, and in their better years, my Parents rarely missed an occasion to get in their car and go. Vegas road-tripping contributed to them replacing their Chrysler 300 sedan three times in two decades as they ran up 120,000-plus miles on a blonde model, a dark blue version, and a slate-grey cruiser.

Las Vegas wasn't their hometown, they had no relatives or friends living there. Still, the city took center-stage in their family and financial lives, and i can't see or think of Vegas without feeling my Parents in the desert air.

They kicked off couplehood in their 50s by getting married in Las Vegas on the second day of September during a Labor Day weekend. My Dad picked the day purposely to avoid encroaching on my 1 September birthdate, but also to keep two of his key life moments in strategically close proximity.

Harrah's Hotel typically served as my Parents' Vegas crash pad. They stayed so often for birthdays, anniversaries, Mother's Day, Father's Day, 4th of July, New Year's, that hotel staff knew them by name. Since i don't drink, gamble or rave, Vegas didn't hook me until my Dad's strategery set us up for dual birthday / anniversary celebrations.

For my inaugural visit, my Parents stepped outside their Harrah's comfort zone and booked us at Paris Hotel, fancy for a Vegas first-timer with its faux-European decor, sky-blue ceiling, and plate-sized crêpes available at all hours. Most importantly, Paris boasted upscale amenities, and i realized i could do Vegas as an introvert and give myself a quality time: a morning walk on an empty Strip for 10,000 steps; a detox day at the spa; dinner with the Parents; then out for art and inspiration at Cirque du Soleil.

When i wanted to track my Parents down, i'd start on the casino floor and typically find my Beloved Momma putting her Baptist church-lady vibes to work, praying over and laying hands on a slot machine. Like, actually rubbing her palms across the screen as the wheels spun. Her blessed touch and hours of unrelenting stamina – she couldn't stay awake in her armchair at home for a 2-hour movie but could sit at the slots from post-buffet dinner until 3 or 4am – helped her bank thousands of dollars and months of free hotel nights from slot machine play. My first trip with them, she took home $7,000.

My Dad's job was to keep her fueled with coffee and snacks, and to hold her up so she didn't fall out when she hit big money. She once dropped her last $25 in a slot, pressed the button, and won $32,000. Security escorted them back to their room that night. So common were her wins, "That ain't nothing new" became the family refrain about her fortune. Her slot winnings paid off one of my Parents' cars, bought them each a Rolex, and handily supplemented their fixed income. Vegas was their side-hustle, and they often came home happy.

As different as we were, my Parents and i found a rhythm together in Vegas. They did their thing, i did my thing, we'd meet for meals, and everyone got to live their best life. Sometimes, we walked and window-shopped. We'd also pile in the car and venture off-Strip to Lucille's for the only barbecue my Dad enjoyed as much as his own.

Over the years, i came to be my most relaxed in Las Vegas, and i have my Parents to thank for so many exceptionally memorable times there. If i wanted to feel them close again, i wouldn't go to the cemetery, i'd go to Vegas. It's the first place my Parents and i experienced how much we could enjoy each other's adult company. It's the last place my Parents and i came together to celebrate as a family. The occasion? Thanksgiving.

/ .-.. --- ...- . /

The way things used to work, my Beloved Momma would sit down at her 8-seat dining room table the first week of November and write out her 3-page shopping list.

Over the next several weeks, she and my Dad would make no fewer than 7 trips to the grocery store, and my Dad (and me, and anyone else who visited in November) would be sent on multiple store runs for various one-off items.

As far as she was concerned, what you had going on in your life was of little import compared to the production she had going on in the kitchen. It wasn't uncommon for me to arrive at my Parents' house road-weary after a 6-hour drive, in dire need of a bio break, only to be sent right back out with a "Go get me ____________." directive before i could unload my luggage.

You could've just come in from running a marathon, and in her honeyed Southern way, she'd likely say, "Since you got your runnin' shoes on, go'n and run over to the store and get me 2 dozen eggs. Go'n now, i got to get these pies in the oven."

With her voice rich and sweet like fresh-baked biscuits and warm maple syrup, you were inclined to submit to her charm and follow even her most bothersome orders.

In contrast, Dad's gravelly voice sounded like Papa Bear complaining about Goldilocks eating his porridge. In his senior years, he kinda resembled an old well-fed grizzly, too. His hair thinned but mostly stayed a fuzzy gray covering on his head. He'd never been able to grow much of a beard, but he kept a goatee of salt-and-pepper scruff on his chin as a manly accessory.

Once retired from the military and freed from mandatory physical training, he refused to exercise in any way, shape, or form. He also really, really enjoyed sleeping like it was a sport or hobby. In his military heyday, the Army's motto had been: "We do more before 9am than some people do all day." My Dad lived this tagline most work mornings of his military life, typically leaving the house before 5am to do god-knows-what before first light. In retirement, he relished a life of languid luxury, sleeping whenever and however long he wanted, morning, noon and night.

His sedentary life thickened his neck to twice its original size, adding several additional rolls between the back of his head and the tops of his shoulders. His back broadened. His belly extended. He went from wearing medium-sized shirts early in his marriage to buttoning up 2XXLs by the end of it. His wife's cooking contributed in good measure to his girth, and Thanksgiving served as a prime example of how he came to be.

A friend who experienced Thanksgiving with my Parents, and who graciously included me for holidays with his family after i buried mine, said of the experience: "From what I remember, there were, like, a thousand things to eat." It's hyperbole, but not by much.

Cooking for Thursday began Monday. The menu held true to their Southern roots:

- Turkey 3 ways: 1 stuffed + baked, 1 seasoned + deep-fried, 1 pan of drumsticks
- a ham garnished with pineapple rings pinned down by hand-placed cloves
- a cafeteria-sized tin of macaroni made with Velveeta and government cheese because that's what melts the best
- a cafeteria-sized tin of baked sweet potatoes with several pounds of butter, several cups of brown sugar, and absolutely no marshmallows
- a cafeteria-sized tin of cornbread dressing seasoned with turkey giblets
- a bread-loaf-sized tin of dressing free of turkey giblets made just for me
    - i refused to learn what giblets are but knew for certain they weren't for me
- a multi-gallon pot of collard greens with ham hocks
- a multi-quarter pot of giblet gravy (nope)
- a dozen cornbread muffins
- 2 dozen deviled eggs
- 6 cans of jellied cranberry sauce
- a baking dish of banana pudding with a Nilla Wafer cookie crust
- a baking dish of peach cobbler with additional pounds of butter
- a 7-Up poundcake and / or a sock-it-to-me cake

- no fewer than 10 sweet potato pies from raw sweet potatoes, hand-peeled by my Beloved Momma, despite her arthritis

If you felt your arteries clog and A1C rise as you read this list, i get that. To offset the indulgence, i signed up for high-intensity workouts from October through December.

Amidst her peeling, prepping, and fussing about, my Beloved Momma phone-chatted, watched soap operas, and sang to Kirk Franklin's "Praise" channel. This sole preset on my Parents' in-home SiriusXM radio played even when they weren't home, filling their house with inspiration and encouragement.

Combine gospel's soulfulness with cinnamon's scent, and you've got Thanksgiving's feel with my Parents.

No one was really invited for the holiday. Folks just knew to arrive. Since my Beloved Momma couldn't know for certain how many people would be coming, she cooked to feed a multi-generational tribe, which in essence is how she started in the kitchen.

The first time she cooked a meal, she liked to recount, was for her Daddy and Momma and several brothers who worked the fields in the Alabama countryside where she grew up. As she told it, one morning at the age of 10, after everybody left for fieldwork, she loaded several pieces of wood into the kitchen stove and fired it up so she could surprise the family when they came in for lunch. She'd been watching her Momma and felt confident she could deliver fried chicken and cornbread. She stood on a stool in front of the stove because she wasn't yet tall enough to reach past the front burners.

Several hours later, her family came in for lunch to find the kitchen table covered with a bedsheet. With the drama of a magician revealing a trick, she pulled back the sheet to reveal her surprise. At this point in her story, she'd chuckle and say: "My half-cooked fried chicken was the worst my Daddy ever ate, but he didn't say so at the time."

Her family's homestead was a simple 1-story 5-room all-wooden farmhouse lifted off the ground by a rickety collection of wooden posts and concrete blocks. Fortunately, she didn't burn the place to the ground lighting kitchen fires and cooking with hot oil.

Maybe because of how she started in the kitchen, my Beloved Momma would say she didn't hardly know how to cook a meal for two. Her culinary talent centered on making comfort food for many and enveloping everyone in a carb-fueled sugar-high embrace.

At its peak, Thanksgiving at my Parents' brought ~50 people into their single-story 1300-square-foot home from noon to midnight. In their family and community, they became legendary for their Thanksgiving feasts, and their table was open to anyone.

As long as you knew how to act.

Because unless you were talking about football, Thanksgiving at my Parents' was no place for your opinions.

The point and purpose of Thanksgiving was to give thanks and revel in all the good: good food, good fun, good company, good conversation, good laughs, a good game of dominoes or cards, and the goodness of being alive.

My Parents' home prominently featured photos of the Obamas. Couldn't stomach their politics? Then don't come by asking after their pie. You didn't need to agree with them. You just didn't need to be going on about it at Thanksgiving.

If you showed up at my Parents' house for the holiday, you needed to know, this was neither the time nor the place to process your pent-up personal grievances. Either you hashed out your differences by early November, or you tabled them 'til early December.

Sometimes, folks showed up who couldn't hardly stand each other, but everybody had a place and plate as long as they didn't start no mess. Anyone who didn't know how to act still got to eat, but they got talked about (sometimes, talked to) post-holiday and didn't get encouraged to come back next year.

Consider the expense and effort it took to travel, the shopping that started weeks prior, days of planning, prepping, and cooking. We didn't sully all the positive energy poured into this time with arguments and upset. Except when it came to hot sauce.

Way before "Hot Ones" debuted on YouTube, i watched many a testosterone-driven, spice-aggressive Thanksgiving newcomer step to my Dad's hot sauce challenge and get smacked down by a tiny taste from a spoon with a bowl no bigger than a raindrop.

Mostly men would gather around my Dad's hot sauce collection discussing particulars, and someone would inevitably insist on sampling the smallest bottle.

My Dad gleefully sent many a grown man fleeing to the bathroom to swear and suffer their burning tongues in private. They'd stumble back into the "told-you-so" crowd all wet-eyed, cheeks flushed, and bravado humbled.

If my Dad could've sorted out hot sauce on his breakfast cereal, he might have (he topped it with fruit cocktail, instead). As it was, he ate hot sauce on nearly everything he ate. A poor man's boy with an 11-sibling family, Dad said they grew up "eatin' a pig from the rooter to the tooter" e.g. hog's head cheese, chitlins, pig's feet, and fried pork skins. For all that, you needed hot sauce.

My hot sauce tolerance is absolute zero, and i used to think the stuff a dangerous way to sear one's insides. Then i learned that the capsaicin compound igniting a pepper's heat also aids gut health by eliminating disease-causing microbes and encouraging beneficial bacteria. Hot sauce likely made it safer to eat a pig, rooter, tooter and all.

When i look closely, i often discover this kind of practical wisdom in my Dad's ways.

The hot sauce challenges also conveniently redirected boisterous energy, which no doubt tamped down potential family disagreements. Anyone who insisted on arguing about anything would unwittingly find themselves arguing about hot sauce, and before they knew what's what, the challenge was on. If you couldn't take heat, you definitely didn't make heat. The hot sauce goings-on were usually as heated as things got.

Another norm that likely helped keep Thanksgiving untroubled: Anyone wanting to drink something stronger than sweet tea or smoke something other than a ham made their way to the backyard through the open garage. It's not like my Parents told people where they could or couldn't imbibe, but people who knew my Parents didn't see them drink or smoke in their own home, and alcohol didn't center in my Parents' everyday or holiday lives. BYOBers and the 420-friendly respected that and claimed their spot at the patio dining table outside, a perk of Thanksgiving celebrated in the desert warmth.

When i still smoked shisha, i brought my hooka pipe home for the holiday and set up on the back patio with the other indulgers. It was fun, that one time. Eventually though, a persistent cough and scratchy throat got me to a doctor who found a grape-sized pleomorphic adenoma bulging from the back of my mouth near my salivary glands.

This 3-out-of-100,000-people unusual kind of tumor typically manifests in women and starts benign, but can get real malignant real quick. Surgery pops a pleomorphic tumor right out, and once removed, they rarely return. But holy wingdings, the pain from a doctor lasering that tumor clean off left me unable to speak above a whisper for 5 days as my throat healed from the scorch. Its message came through loudly and clearly.

After that, i dumped my hookah pipe, stopped smoking shisha, and never told my Parents what happened. The situation had been settled, i wanted it to stay that way.

/ .-.. --- ...- . /

My Parents both smoked cigarettes, just not in their house or cars. Dad smoked while pacing the driveway. My Beloved Momma smoked in the garage. Or Vegas, they both smoked when in Vegas. And drank a bit, too.

This one time, i got to meet blues legend B.B. King because my Parents' profusive casino game-play netted several complimentary concert tickets and champagne, a fancy treat for folks living on Social Security and retirement wages. We got backstage because the pretty face of a family friend caught the attention of a bouncer minding the door. Lit on free bubbly, my Beloved Momma giggled uncontrollably and leaned on my arm as we waited an hour to get Mr. King's autograph. My Dad held himself up against the back wall near the buffet table and consumed all the cheese and crackers on hand.

By the time i ushered them safely back into their hotel room, my completely sober adult self felt as if i'd spent an evening chaperoning teenagers at a 1960s high school dance.

My Beloved Momma knew she couldn't hardly hold her liquor. My Dad knew drinking didn't make him a better person. In the decades of our lives together, this night was once of only twice i experienced them inebriated, the other being a Vegas New Year's Eve during which i left them to their own devices and got to bed by 10:30pm to be up early and have the spa mostly to myself. Life in that way was calm, safe and peacefully predictable with them, at least when it came to alcohol.

But smoking? Sigh. Neither of my Parents could give it up, no matter that it actively worsened my Dad's COPD, or the heart attack my Beloved Momma had in her 60s during bingo night at the local Senior Center.

Dad called to tell me. With all the sensitivity of an Army general recounting battle plans, he started with the bad news. Standing in my kitchen unsuspecting and unprepared, my knees for-real buckled and nearly gave way when he said "heart attack" and i had to grab the counter to keep upright.

Thank goodness he finished with a simple "she alright now" and praised the Lord that the Senior Center was across the street from the local hospital.

My thanks went to mindful city planners that the ambulance only had to wail its way from one side of the road to the other to gather her up and get her to emergency care.

She refused to go back to bingo at the Senior Center. But she didn't give up smoking. Neither did my Dad. Despite efforts with nicotine gum. No matter how much i pressed.

At the time, i didn't know my Parents coped with anxiety, a mental health challenge i also didn't know how to recognize because it hadn't been a life affliction for me. My Beloved Momma's 8-day hospital stay after kidney surgery pulled back the curtain on the uncontrollable fear and worry she couldn't self-medicate or mask without smoking.

Her doctor wanted her on anti-anxiety meds day and night, and was taken aback when i took that decision out of his hands. The medication sedated her so heavily, we would never have gotten her functional enough to get her out of her hospital bed. Despite our tense negotiation, the doctor moved past me questioning his expertise and agreed that since my presence calmed her, i could stay with her 12 hours a day every day until she could be discharged. She'd only need to take anti-anxiety meds after 8pm to quell the panic attacks she'd been having throughout the night.

Before i could clearly see all their health issues, the heart attack jolted me into realizing i likely would not have them much past their 70s, so i made a point, no matter where in the world i found myself or who i might be with or what i might be doing, to get myself back to their desert town and spend Thanksgiving with my Parents and all their fixin's.

And so it went for the better part of 15 years until 2019.

We got my Beloved Momma out of the hospital by mid-November that year, too late to host the holiday in their way. There was so much to be thankful for still, so this time, we headed to Vegas for the smoked turkey meal at Lucille's.

The small family contingent, just 8 of us, included 2 favorite cousins who were close to my Parents. They left their primary families and traditions and flew from Alabama to be with us. We spoke of how they felt called to be with my Parents this particular holiday: "Ain't no tellin' how many of these we have left with them." Turns out, just that one.

Good times with my Parents started in Vegas and ended in Vegas. They are buried and honored in the cemetery. They are alive for me in Las Vegas.

/ .-.. --- ...- . /

One of the few places outside their home as central to my Parents' lives as Las Vegas was their 40-ish-member church of mostly Black folks and retired military seniors. Out of respect, i'd join Sunday service when in town, but i only had so much capacity for condemnatory religious preachings. The day their Pastor went on a tangent from the pulpit about the abomination of gay sex and gay people, i walked my Parents to their car, told them i needed to have a word, and headed back inside for the last time.

As i closed my Beloved Momma's car door, i saw the wide-eyed concern on her face and promised i wouldn't do or say anything to embarrass her or my Dad.

It didn't feel necessary to start the half-hour conversation with their pastor by telling him how offensive i found his sermon as a gay person. Sitting in his office after his sermon said enough. Instead, i asked what was so personally material for him about gay people that, apropos of nothing, he felt compelled to preach on them.

Eventually he came out from behind the Bible to reveal he'd been sexually assaulted by several older boys while in middle school. His confidently instructive preacher's voice cracked with the revelation of his trauma. His eyes couldn't meet mine as he spoke of what he had suffered. He called it a "gay sex" experience.

What he experienced wasn't gay sex. It was rape. It was an exertion of dominant force. Until our conversation, he hadn't discussed this violation with anyone who delineated the difference. My breath caught in my throat, gripped with grief as i took in his story. Harmful as i found his religious rhetoric, i deeply felt his hurt.

The pastor talked of the terror he survived, the rage still in his heart, his confusion at the cruelty. In all his professional Christian training and teaching, he had not yet found forgiveness for the violators who hurt him, or forgiveness for God failing to protect him.

So often i see people debilitated and imprisoned by an inability to forgive. This pastor, still suffering, had not found release and peace for himself, and it showed in his pulpit.

We ended on an amicable note as i suggested he reconsider the impact he could have in the position of power he now held. "You don't know who's out in your congregation, coming to your church in need of support, salvation, getting an earful of condemnation instead. You OK with your life work possibly contributing to a young person's suicide?"

He said he'd give this some thought, and he'd pray on it.

Also, i told him that i'd never step foot in his church again, not so much because of his condemnation, but because no one, including my Parents, had stood up to protest it.

The pastor stopped by my Parents' for cake and coffee later that day, as he often did on Sunday afternoons. After i answered the door, welcomed him in, and got him settled with his first cup, i went back to watching football with no animosity and nothing further to say. Gratitude and respect for my Parents led me through our conversation with an imperative to say my piece, but without disrupting their peace.

Church mattered to them, and even church that didn't refute and rebuke condemnation (which, sidenote, i find ironic considering the horrific condemned-Jesus ordeal at the crux of Christianity), still contributed to my Parents being fundamentally good people.

Church gave them somewhere to be of service, to be part of something larger than themselves, to contribute constructively as elders, and to cultivate their peace-of-mind.

/ .-.. --- ...- . /

My Beloved Momma started every normal day of her life with a morning read of her heavily highlighted and annotated Bible. She wasn't formally educated beyond high school, but she was a scholar of faith. She Bible-studied and ruminated on the Word like she was prepping for final exams. In various nooks and crannies of her home, one could find Bible verses scribbled on scraps of paper as she regularly captured thoughts and heavenly guidance to trust in the Lord, rejoice in life, and uplift others.

According to her Bible, the sincere and humble prayer of a true believer ascends to heaven and makes a difference. My Beloved Momma took this literally and seriously, and given the impact of her prayers, it did seem like she might have a hotline to Jesus.

Once she told me, "I'ma pray for you to have patience," and i was aghast. No doubt this was a legit prayer request, as i notoriously lacked patience and had often insisted that i'd be patient when i'm dead and not a moment before. Getting called out by my Beloved Momma wasn't the issue, it's what she planned to do about it that scared me.

"Don't be prayin' for me to have patience!" i demanded. "Why not?" she asked.

"Because if you pray for me to have patience, then i'ma need to deal with messed-up situations that require me to practice patience, and i don't need aggravation in my life."

She smiled at me undeterred and said with her sweet Southern church-lady conviction: "I'ma pray for you anyway."

Shortly thereafter, the 2008 financial crisis hit, my job disappeared, my bank account dried up, and it took 11 months to regain my financial footing. Student loan and credit card companies harangued me on the daily, offering ample opportunity to either lose my mind or develop patience.

Opting to explore what patience could offer, i learned its ingredients include:

- self-control to manage my emotions and my mouth
- tolerance and composure to cope with frustration and dismay
- willingness to respect the moment and meet it as-is as best i could

My patience-initiation felt like a baptism by fire. Some might call it mere coincidence, this happenstance arriving on the heels of my Beloved Momma's prayer request.

Meh, probably, but also, possibly not.

If her prayers got me into hard spots, Dad's prayers likely helped get me out of them. My Dad prayed for me daily because he wanted me to have a good life, but per usual, he didn't share details. His prayer skills developed after he finally married for love, and he borrowed from his wife's faith until his was strong enough to stand beside hers.

Together, my Parents' prayers offered protective cover and high-powered assistance. Their conviction and its efficacy were bolstered by generations of their ancestors who used prayer and faith as survival and life-affirming tools: for themselves, for those they loved, and for people they didn't know who were nonetheless material to their lives.

This is partly why my Parents had pictures of the Obamas in their home: They didn't just admire the family, they also prayed for them.

Across the decades, i saw my Parents make an abundant life from modest resources and miraculous serendipities. Like buying a home with no down payment because they rented from a homeowner who unexpectedly got military orders for Alaska and trusted my Parents' faith-driven integrity enough to let them rent-to-own.

Or, having a heart attack right across the street from a hospital. Or, having cancerous tumors concentrate in one removable kidney. Or, repeatedly beating the odds in Vegas.

No, i'm neither religious nor superstitious, but i can't deny the creative life force that seemed to work in their favor. Their prayers were positive contributions to that force, and a positive declaration of its power.

My Beloved Momma's unshakable faith and belief in care and prayer transformed into living, breathing tangible things that spilled over just about everyone she encountered.

Once when i visited my Parents, i caught a wicked case of bronchitis and they took me to the local emergency room. As we waited, a family came in visibly distraught, with much crying and concern as EMTs wheeled one of their kin into intensive care. Without a moment's hesitation, My Beloved Momma left her seat, waded into the middle of this family, guided them into a hand-holding circle, and led them in prayer.

Coughing, tight-chested, and bewildered, i asked my Dad, "Does she know them?!"

My gravelly-voiced Pops drawled nonchalantly, "She don't need to know them. She does stuff like that all the time."

Friend or stranger didn't matter, if a person was in need, she wanted to be there. When she could do something for you, like take you to the hospital, she did. And when there wasn't much she could do for you, she prayed.

Living in her light, when i now find myself in a moment with someone who's in distress, i ask if it's OK for us to breathe together, and if yes, i take 3 breaths with them - deep inhale, hold at the top, long exhale. It's the closest i get to rounding up a prayer circle.

As a longtime church lady, she stayed honest about how she struggled with me being gay, and i told her she could struggle all she wanted. She was still my Beloved Momma no matter what. In the course of life, as she came to know my girlfriends and queer friends, as she fed and hosted them, shared stories and laughed with them, enjoyed their good company, saw how much i loved them and how much they loved me, she came around, saying: "It's just about love, ain't it? I do understand if it's about love."

My Dad seemed wholly unbothered by and never took issue with me being gay. He was more confused about how i didn't own a television and what i did for a living. When i worked in digital media, i told him simply that i worked on the internet, and he told a favorite cousin that i was *in charge* of the internet. To which my cousin replied: "No wonder we don't talk on the phone. Who got time if you runnin' the entire internet."

In his hyperbole, i heard my Dad being proud of me even though my life didn't make much sense to him. Announcing plans to do my PhD, for example, required explaining a PhD to my Dad. No one he knew had done one, so he had no reference point for it.

Post-PhD, my Dad framed and featured the degree in his home alongside his wedding pictures. From then on, when he brought me to his doctor appointments, he'd tell staff that i was also a doctor, and i'd need to explain, actually, i'm not *that* kind of doctor, and he'd inevitably say, "Well, whichever kinda doctor you are, you're a doctor to me."

From whom i loved to what i did for a living, my Parents didn't need to understand or agree with me to support and pray for me. It's a most extraordinary truth about these ordinary people who made so much from so little and left a legacy of unconditional grace that no cemetery or headstone can reflect or contain.

That's why these parents are my Parents, with a capital P.

They are the most important adults of my life.

They are my Love Heroes.

Love Stories

- *Do you have Love Heroes? If so, who and why them? If not, what's that story?*

- *Got any loving traditions that you keep up with the people who are your people? If so, what do your traditions do for you, how do they feed you? If not, thoughts?*

2. FROM BEGINNING . . .

Forever together in their final resting place, my Parents initially found their way back to each other in their 50s, fittingly, at a funeral.

They hadn't seen each other since their teens when they'd been each other's first love. My Beloved Momma's family lived in the country. Dad's family lived in town. With their birthdays just 3 months apart, they met in school and by the time they both turned 17, my Dad knew she was The One.

Her momma, after meeting my Dad, had proclaimed and prophesied to her daughter: "There go yo' husband." But my Beloved Momma hadn't been so sure.

It was hard to hear sage advice with the star player from the school's basketball team also in ardent pursuit of her affections. This fella looked to be someone who could get somewhere. He could get a scholarship at a college beyond Alabama. He could open the door to prospects and adventure. She could step into a whole new life with him.

Dad worked a delivery job at a pharmacy in his late teens and had no obvious talents. How would he get them out of the South? What kind of future could he offer?

A woman's choice of husband could dramatically change her fortunes, especially when women didn't come from money, couldn't get bank loans or credit cards without a man involved, and were hard-pressed to make their own opportunities. My Beloved Momma found herself calculating between her head and her heart. "I loved yo' Daddy," she said of the time, but back then, she couldn't afford to trust that love could be enough.

My Dad squared up to the competition and laid out his proposal: Either she marry him, or he would follow an older brother into the Army and leave for Vietnam. Love or war. Those were his options.

As part of his proposal, he spent his hard-earned cash gifting my Beloved Momma a record player and a box of Whitman's Sampler chocolates.

My Dad got about town on a motorcycle for his delivery job, and on one of his off-days, he rode it out to the country to see about her answer. He arrived at her family home to find her sitting on the front porch with the basketball star. A window had been opened so they could hear music from the record player. The Whitman box had been sampled.

"Yo' Daddy got off his motorbike, saw what he saw, walked up on the porch, went right on past us into the house, and without speaking a word, unplugged that record player, scooped it up with the chocolate box, put 'em in the crate on his bike, and rode away."

Astonished a fight hadn't ensued, i asked my Dad about this. There's no way this old bear of a man who could swear like a drunken sailor had ridden off without cussing them out. "Wasn't nothing more to say," my Dad confirmed. "But I sure as shit wasn't gon' have her using that record player and eatin' my chocolates with some other man."

Imagine the motorcycle ride back to town. Rattling across bone-jarring dirt roads, wind and bugs slapping you in the face, the pain of rejection twisting in your chest, the sickly dejection of not being enough for the one person you love.

Imagine having no way to process or alchemize your rejection and loss. There's no therapist to help you hold your heartache in a healthy way, no space to normalize a 19-year-old young man's emotional vulnerability or validate his emotional pain.

At a time when American men skipped off to college or Canada or got medical waivers to avoid the draft, Dad made good on his ultimatum. He walked his nascent and injured manhood into a military recruiting office to enlist in the Army and get the hell away from heartbreak. His sole tattoo, ***Fly Boy*** in cursive script across his right forearm, marked his post-training readiness to jump from military helicopters into jungle warfare.

Actually, as many times as i'd seen my Dad's tattoo, i still had to fact-check which arm he'd inked. We can spend a lifetime looking at someone and still not see all the details.

/ -... . --. .. -. -. .. -. --. /

Fly Boy returned from his first tour of combat duty to find his
first love had moved West and moved on. He settled and married
a different hometown girl whom he didn't really love and who
didn't really love him. Given the times they were in, love under-
standably took a backseat to pragmatism.

Rioting had beset their town after President John F. Kennedy sent in troops to remove Governor George Wallace from the state university's steps. Vowing "segregation now, segregation tomorrow, segregation forever" for Alabama, the governor blockaded the door to keep Black students from registering for an education at the all-White school.

Setting love aside, Fly Boy sought a companion to roam the world as a military spouse. She wanted out of Alabama by any means necessary. Their union offered each enough substance and reason to say "I do."

He returned from a second tour of combat duty saturated in the PTSD of war-making and bound to a woman with violent compulsions that matched his own. Unchecked trauma and combustible emotions warped their union into a battleground. Companions in arms, the two of them proceeded to have a terrifying marriage for the next 23 years.

"I thought about yo' Daddy over the years, and when I got divorced, I asked about him, but he still had his wife, and I didn't wanna get mixed up in that," my Beloved Momma told me. So she let it be, waited patiently, and trusted in the Lord, like she always did.

While she weathered her own sagas, she never let go of ties to Dad's family, and the family held on to her, too. Among the older folks from their small country town, family connections outlived break-ups and weathered time. If love pulled you into the family, you could be in for life, and you'd know about folks. You'd hear who moved here and there, who got married, who had a baby, who got divorced, who passed on, when and where funeral services were taking place.

This is how my Beloved Momma came to be at the funeral for the daughter of the older brother my Dad had followed into the Army. Somebody had loved my Beloved Momma enough to keep her in the family. And thus, she could find herself sitting in just the right place at the right time for her head to catch up to her heart.

/ -... . --. .. -. -. .. -. --. /

Funerals in my Black family typically include a repast, from the Latin word *repascere*: *re-* expressing intensive force and the verb *pascere* meaning "to feed". You can cry, you can shout, you can throw an emotional fit at a Black funeral. But the one offense you cannot commit is running out of food at the repast. It is indeed a big feed, like a mini-Thanksgiving, with lots of storytelling, reminiscing, celebrating, and picture-taking.

Photos at a funeral may sound odd, but oftentimes, these working folks would go long spells without visiting faraway family, so many a family reunion happened at a funeral.

Grief certainly was on hand. Weeping and wailing abounded. But if folks cared enough to be at your funeral, love was also present, and a repast was the time when everyone basked in love for you and for each other.

My Parents stumbled upon each other during the love part of the funeral, at the repast.

On the way to finalizing his divorce, Dad didn't miss this opportunity for a do-over. For years to come, i heard him recount and relish their meet-cute as a real-life romantic moment that changed his life for good. "I had my hands full carrying a cooler of sodas when I saw her outta the corner of my eye. I called her name, she looked at me, and I said: 'Don't go nowhere. I'll be right back.' I went and threw that cooler down as fast as I could, came back, and sat right down next to her. That's where I been ever since."

That's where he stayed through her last day, in a chair pulled close to her hospital bed in their home so he could rest a hand on her. Head bowed, chin settled on his rising and falling chest, eyes closed, he sat beside her for hours, like a slumbering guardian bear.

The first time i visited my Parents to see them in their new home, my Dad and i went to Walmart, and within minutes, my Beloved Momma got a phone call about her husband running around town with a woman who was way too tall and much too young for him.

People doubted my Parents loved each other as thoroughly and genuinely as they did, but i have receipts. My Beloved Momma kept letters my Dad sent her in the early days of their middle-aged courtship, when they still lived apart. Her replies weren't among their effects, but i gleaned from his responses, in handwriting neatly ordered on lined paper, glimpses of what she'd told him and the feelings they shared.

There is no blame, anger, or retrospecting about the past. If there was lingering hurt to pardon, it isn't mentioned. They both had their hearts set on a future that'd be brighter together, and they could hardly wait to get to it.

Cue the classic love jams from back in their day: "Save the Last Dance" by the Drifters; "Wonderful World" by Sam Cooke; "Will You Still Love Me Tomorrow" by the Shirelles. My Parents were youngsters again, falling back into love with teenaged abandon.

They were also middle-aged and mired in life challenges.

Dad had relieved himself of military duty but still needed to work because, though he'd been good about making money, he'd been bad at saving it. So his days continued to start at 5am as he got underway on his hourlong commute to a contractor security job at a military base.

My Beloved Momma, meanwhile, lived money-tight and hand-to-mouth on disability checks after a workplace accident severely damaged a foot. Multiple surgeries and physical therapy didn't alter the facts of her condition but did make walking bearable.

Just as my Beloved Momma struggled to care for herself despite (and because of) years spent caretaking others, Dad struggled to live a well-managed life post-military despite (and because of) all his years with imposed military discipline.

Without an external force structuring his life choices, health challenges emerged from poor decision-making. In the midst of falling-in-love-again time with all its happiness and hopefulness, his stomach exploded from diverticulitis, an inflamed infection in his digestive tract. He'd been unwilling to address the telltale abdominal pain and nausea, so his body revolted, and Fly Boy found himself in another helicopter, this time on the way to emergency surgery that stitched him together from sternum to waistline in an effort to save his life.

My Beloved Momma lived several hours away without a car, and didn't have anyone who could drive her to him. She borrowed as much money as she could from everyone she could and took the most expensive taxi ride she'd make in her life. She said it may have been a mistake to tell the cab driver how much money she had for how far she needed to travel, but she did so anyway. He drove her to within 2 miles of the hospital, stopped the cab, and said that's as far as he would go. He took all the money she had and let her out to walk the rest of the way. Which she did. Uphill. On one good foot.

Her devotion found its mate in my Dad. As soon as he was well enough, they married.

/ -... . --. .. -. -. .. -. --. /

He provided for her, maintaining a steady paycheck and turning all of it over to her management, save for a modest allowance of walking-around money in his pocket.

She cared for him, kept him well-dressed and well-fed, and leveraged her caretaking experience with diabetes to manage his blood-sugar tracking and insulin shots.

They fussed over inconsequential things, like how long it took my Beloved Momma to get out of the house because her appearance had to be just so. This required stops at 4 mirrors between the bedroom and front door to primp her natural curls into place.

But they didn't argue or fight. They kissed and hugged, even in public, and they lived 'til death did them part. The stuff of their

togetherness – love, service, prayer, faith, commitment, celebration, thanksgiving – made life a richer place for all of us to be.

Through the financial crisis, when it took so long to find my way through uncertainty (possibly due to that Patience prayer request), my Dad would say: "We ain't got much, but as long as we're here, you know where home is." To be so firmly anchored in their love was a treasure i did not take for granted. Off-and-on while unmarried and without children, i lived with my Parents, somewhat out of necessity, but mainly out of choice.

With them was where i wanted to be. It was a gift to be with them while we were all well enough to enjoy each other and sane enough to ensure an enjoyable time.

Though much harder, it was also a gift to be with them when they died.

Togetherness

- *Who's someone you've spent a lifetime looking at but still haven't seen all the details? Remember, that someone could be you. Whomever this person is, what's one thing you don't yet know about them that you'd like to?*

- *What is your stuff of togetherness? Whether it's real or ideal, whether you currently have it or you don't, what does being "together" mean for you?*

----

3. . . . TO END

When my Beloved Momma was first tested for and diagnosed with kidney cancer, i booked a same-day flight, got to the hospital where she'd been admitted, found her room, pushed past my Dad, climbed into her twin bed, and enveloped her in my arms.

A year later, it was she and i once again in a twin-sized hospital bed, this one in her home. My Dad needed a break, so i'd sent him off with family friends, then climbed into her bed to hold her as she sobbed, "I don't wanna go!" and railed against her last days.

With her back pressed to my chest, i drew in and released deep, methodical breaths. There was nothing i could say, and it was all i could think to do.

Eventually, she collected herself. She said there wasn't no more use crying about it. The Lord had given her most of what she'd asked for: a loving husband, her family, good friends, plenty of good times. She hadn't won the big-money lottery despite playing every week, but she'd otherwise gotten from life all she could have wanted.

She also said she could feel the empty space inside where her kidney had been. The hole ached, but she knew the Lord had put all the hardness she went through in that kidney and took it all out of her. She'd had a chance to trust her heart and choose love, and it had all worked out in the end.

Now it was time to go.

She then began telling me how she wanted things arranged. Most importantly, she wanted to spend eternity wearing her "partials" – shorthand for the dental implants that replaced her 12 front teeth. She'd always been highly concerned about people seeing her without her partials, so i had to promise and swear i would not let that happen.

My Beloved Momma spent her final 4 days bedridden and unable to move her legs, the energy slowly draining from her body. My first order of business was to re-hire in-home care for professional support with keeping her as clean and comfortable as possible. It is truly impressive how quickly an experienced care provider can swap bedsheets out from under an adult body lying in a twin bed. My Dad and i couldn't manage together what one person could achieve when they actually knew what they were doing.

In-home care also trained me on the fundamentals of looking after her e.g. washing her hair, bathing her, and brushing her teeth in ways that didn't soak her bed.

As long as she wanted to eat, my Dad cooked whatever she requested. She said she had a taste for collard greens, and Dad cooked a Thanksgiving-sized pot, of which she ate a few spoonfuls. It was her last meal, a fine country send-off for a fine country girl.

With the basics handled, she and Dad spent their time together sleeping. They also worked on practical matters. She walked him through how to use the high-efficiency washing machine, which he hadn't touched in the 10 years since we'd all gone to Sears together and i'd bought it to help them save water and money. At one point, i saw Dad headed down the hall with a toilet brush and a bottle of toilet cleaner in hand. Apparently, my Beloved Momma had been instructing him on how to tidy up the loo.

My time with her was spent laughing and singing, retelling our favorite stories and jokes, and playing her favorite gospel songs.

Being with her in her final days and hours was a slow process that happened quickly, like watching the sun disappear beyond the horizon. You see it happening for a while, then just like that, it's done. One evening she could eat, the next morning, she couldn't consume anything more than ice chips and sips of water. By nightfall, she'd stopped talking but could still turn her head and watch my face as i stood over her reciting the poetry of the 23rd Psalm from her Bible:

The Lord is my shepherd; I shall not want; Yea, though I walk through the valley of the shadow of death, I will fear no evil: for thou art with me.

As evening wore on, her body began to tremble incessantly, her golden-brown skin took on an ashen pallor, she couldn't open her eyes. My Dad was powerless, bereft.

It was time to call on the services of hospice, low-to-no-cost specialized care that looks to reduce pain and suffering for people approaching death. From all i've seen, dying is hard work. Hospice can help ease the transition for patients and their families.

Gently, i approached my Dad. "Pop, she might be in pain, she might be suffering. We don't want her to suffer. Hospice can give her morphine; they can help if she's in pain. But she's your wife. What do you think we should do?"

In a voice so small, so plaintive, so helpless, i didn't recognize it as his, my Dad looked down at his house slippers and asked, "What do *you* think we should do?" Ah, i see, *this* is why my Parents had made me her health care proxy. Dad could not make the final call. He'd let go of her once. He could not let go of her again.

/ . -. -.. /

Hospice didn't have a nurse available who could attend to my late-evening SOS as soon as i wanted, but they promised to send someone by 11am the next day.

My Dad parked himself in his bedside chair the whole of the night, i took over at dawn. By 9am, her breathing shallowed, her chest barely moved. Hospice had not yet arrived.

Using her cellphone, i began dialing people who would want to say goodbye, starting with her siblings. Initially they were furious, in denial, yelling that i get her to a hospital. This was May 2020, peak COVID, when no one could linger at a hospital unless they were on duty or on their deathbed. If i took her to a hospital, she'd be admitted, none of us would be able to be with her there, and she would surely die alone.

Absolutely not. There was no way i would let my Beloved Momma who cared for so many die with no one at her side.

"It's too late for the hospital," i told them. "She's leaving. You can waste time yelling at me, or you can say goodbye. If you want, i'll hold the phone to her ear. She'll hear you. Tell her what she means to you. Tell her how much you love her."

Word quickly got out, and a cacophony of activity ensued.

Faster than i could call, people started ringing her cellphone, Dad's cellphone, their landline. People came to the house and sat vigil with Dad at the dining room table while i juggled devices, popping out of her room to give folks context and a minute to collect themselves, then popping back in to put a phone to her ear.

Inspired by interviewer James Lipton from his long-running *Inside the Actor's Studio* talkshow, i once asked my Beloved Momma a version of a question James asked his famous guests over 277 episodes: "When you get to Heaven, what's the first thing you want to hear God say when you arrive at the Pearly Gates?"

James began his question with "if" and left room for doubt. My Beloved Momma didn't doubt for a moment where she'd be headed. Neither did anyone who loved her.

This was long before her dying day, her leaving wasn't on our minds, and i only asked because i admired her faith and wanted to know what she'd say. Though she'd never seen the show and hadn't anticipated the question, she didn't pause a moment before quoting "Well done, my good and faithful Servant" from Matthew 25:21 in her Bible.

My Beloved Momma wanted to know that her life had pleased the Lord. She wanted to hear words of affirmation.

Baptist Pastor Gary Chapman identified words of affirmation, as well as acts of service, physical touch, quality time and receiving gifts as *The 5 Love Languages.* He reportedly based the love languages on insights gained from thousands of counseling hours with couples on how they express and receive love. He turned the work into a book, and the book turned him into a best-selling author.

Though Pastor Gary first published about love languages in 1992, i didn't learn of them until the 20-teens, and i doubt my Beloved Momma ever knew of them or she might have required all of us to give her more gifts. Still, as much as she adored jewelry and purses, she knew nothing from the material world could pass with her into Heaven.

But a life of good and faithful service? Well, that can be written into eternity.

If the Lord affirmed her life of service, she could rest in peace.

None of these ideas lived anywhere near the forefront of my mind when i started dialing people to share their affirming words with her. Phone calls aren't typically a prescribed remedy for end-of-life situations, not that i'd experienced anyway. Usually, it's a healthy dose of morphine that helps quiet a body enough for its animating spirit to find release.

But i had no morphine on hand, no idea when hospice would arrive, and i felt a frantic push to do something useful as i watched her frail body violently shake the way we do when we're unbearably cold. Unbeknownst to me, that casual conversation inspired by a talkshow question about hearing from the Lord had coalesced into a useful instinct.

Running on this instinct helped shape my Beloved Momma's final hours into a lovefest.

Over and over during 50+ phone calls, family and friends blessed her with "well done" words of affirmation for her care, nurturing, support and love. People poured so much affirmation into her, morphine proved unnecessary. An overflow of her love language provided the escape velocity my Beloved Momma – our Beloved Mother – needed to shake off her mortal coil and pass from this realm into whatever might be next.

She had a loved one's voice in her ear and my hand on the center of her chest when she gasped a handful of rasping inhales and exhales that sounded like she might be choking. Before i could sort what to do, her gasping stopped, her chest fell still, and quietly, she was gone.

/ . -. -.. /

A hole tore in the fabric of the Universe, i thought it might swallow up my Dad. In some ways, it did, but in other ways, he surprised me with his resilience, reminding me of the Fighter in him.

For one thing, he rather preferred to visit the cemetery and wanted me (and only me) to travel 6 hours into town, then drive 4 hours round-trip to stand graveside with him.

Several people offered to take him to the cemetery more often, but he'd refuse and insist on waiting until i could take him to the one place i had no desire to go. Knowing he wouldn't have words to communicate why he needed this, i simply went with him.

We didn't need to understand each other to support each other.

Looking back and beyond my own resistance, it's obvious to me now. My Dad longed for our family. He reached for us in the last place we could gather. At the graveside, we were reunited, as together as we could be.

He also knew he'd be joining her in that grave at some point, another poignant detail we didn't discuss in all the hours we spent driving to and from the cemetery.

One of our visits, i noticed near my Parents' gravesite a headstone for a "Loving Wife" who had died 2 months before my Beloved Momma. According to this headstone, that woman's husband died just a few months after she did.

Pointing this out to my Dad, i said: "You know, it's not unusual, this kind of timing with longtime spouses who don't know how to live without each other." The most my bear of Dad ever said on the matter was: "Hmmph, I ain't in no hurry."

/ . -. -.. /

My Dad's first year without his wife began just as he turned 78. All things considered, he held up OK. He initially suppered on cans of clam chowder, but i introduced him to an easy-to-make meals delivery service, and he got on board with light prep for diverse dinners. He pricked his finger daily to draw the drop of blood needed to track his AlC, and to this day i still have voicemails from him calling with updates on his blood sugar.

Back in his early 70s, Dad rallied his septuagenarian former military mates to establish a Veterans Park in their town. A lack of fundraising momentum thwarted the effort, but the City nonetheless honored him with a commemorative gold-plated plaque inscribed with a proclamation lauding his community commitment.

He got the plaque and a moment of shine during a City Council meeting, with folks stepping to the podium to say good words and the Council embracing him in group photos. The plaque now hangs in my home. In its polished gleam, i can still see my Dad standing to receive it, beckoning his wife to come be at his side.

Despite a plethora of health conditions, my Dad continued to get about his life with that commitment to serving his community.

He took himself to church most Sundays. He recruited members to the local Veterans Support Group that he'd co-founded. He hosted visits from people young and old who called him Brother, Uncle, Papa, and Friend.

Each evening for the first 6 months, i'd call him and we'd take 3 deep breaths together to close out the day. We got Zoom downloaded to his antiquated iPhone 6 (he wouldn't upgrade for fear of losing his photos), and he figured out how to participate in an online weekly grief group. There he introduced our breathing ritual and took charge of leading his fellow mourners through the practice.

With regulated steadiness guiding his days, it seemed like he might live to roughly 112.

By year 2 on his own, signs begin to appear that his comorbidities might be taking a toll. The summer of that year, he experienced an episode of diabetic delirium which i wrote off to being outside his regular rhythm visiting family in the South. Back home, though, he experienced 5 more episodes in the next 6 months.

A middle-aged brother of my Dad's had moved in with him by this time, and whenever i saw his number come up on my phone, i came to expect an ambulance was on its way to my Dad's house.

When the call came in December of that year, i got on the phone with attending paramedics and implored them to do all they legally could to get my Dad admitted to the hospital. Thankfully they obliged, and a doctor with time to attend to my Dad recognized the exacerbated interplay of his diabetes and his heart disease.

The doctor kept my Dad for a few days and kept me informed of my Dad's condition and care needs, with the exception of one critical detail.

Home from the hospital, Dad called to say i needed to ring a phone number the doctor had given him. No further context was provided. It turned out to be a hospice referral.

"Wait, what?!" were my first words to the care manager assigned to support my Dad.

Assuring me, no, my Dad wasn't yet on the verge of passing away, the care manager explained how hospice gets involved when a doctor determines health conditions can no longer be effectively treated at a hospital. In these cases, hospice doesn't so much oversee the quality of impending death. Instead, they help manage quality of life with services to stabilize and support people at home and keep them out of the hospital.

My Dad got home nursing visits, chaplain home check-ins, and a social worker who became his in-home therapist. At 79, precisely 60 years after his first heartbreak, he finally had safe space and self-granted permission to process his loss and heartache.

That first year on his own, my Dad's difficulties had been manageable, less noticeable. By his third year of widowhood, the challenges were perpetual and inescapable.

He lamented the chronic pain in his overburdened joints. He resented the health-related loss of his freedom to live exactly as he preferred.

He called off the deep-breaths ritual we'd continued off-and-on for a couple of years by telling me he just didn't feel like breathing.

He greeted each morning with thanks to the Lord for another day, but his unmitigated PTSD and anxiety agitated him into grumping and grousing for the whole of it.

He also clearly missed the love he'd lost. Sometimes, i'd find him at the dining room table or kitchen sink bent-over sobbing, and i'd lean against him and rub his back until his tears ebbed. Sometimes, i'd find him sitting on the edge of his bed, immobile with sadness, staring into nothing. Once i heard him talking out loud in an otherwise empty room and asked: "Dad, who are you talking to?" He told me he was talking to his wife.

If his old age had become this hard, uncomfortable, lonely, i wondered, why doesn't he just go already? Why stay? Not because i didn't appreciate the relevance of his life, but because i couldn't understand how he could stand suffering. That anyone puts up with suffering utterly confounds me. Personally, i have no tolerance for it. Suffering for me quickly leads to despair, and despair is a spiraling danger zone that i do well to avoid.

All my life, i've been praised for the courage to heal, but my healing hasn't come from bravery. Truth be told, it's come on the run from suffering.

My Dad seemed to thrive on suffering. Fighters need a fight, i suppose, and suffering served as an apt nemesis. He effectively complained his way from day to day and lived to celebrate his 80th birthday with a weekend of parties, cakes, and decorative fanfare.

In grumpiness and gratitude, he lived another 6 months, a period i found particularly crazy-making because, no matter how much his care escalated, somehow my Dad remained unconvinced that he was on the decline.

With advancing glaucoma, he wanted to drive long distances and at night; i had to talk him out of it. Plumbing in both bathrooms of his home required complete replacement, but he wanted to tough it out and not relocate during the repair; i had to talk him into it.

An overwatered peace lily from my Beloved Momma's funeral service succumbed to rot, throwing off a stench so vile, my nose and throat erupted in allergic reaction after one day of exposure. How Dad lived with this toxicity remains beyond comprehension, but he complained mightily when i relocated the rancid plant to an outside trash bin.

His grievances came in large part from grieving the pile-up of losses he'd accumulated in his inexplicably long life - his wife, health, vitality, mobility. The future was coming to an end for him. He thrashed against this reality. Most days, i had it in me to care for him unconditionally without absorbing his emotional weight. Some days, i had to call upon all the patience my Beloved Momma had prayed into me to cope with his fight.

/ . -. -.. /

It didn't occur to me to pray for my Parents when they were alive and together. They were so well-stocked in the faith department, they didn't need my contributions. But after my Beloved Momma left, it became time to step up and tap into positive vibes.

Prayer for me is action-focused. It's a positive declaration to influence the future. In circumstances too complex to figure or configure on my own, prayer marshals and amplifies my intentions. If serendipity is required, if the machinations are many, if the stakes are high: these are my thresholds for prayer.

As mentioned, i'm not religious, so prayer for me doesn't involve the Lord. My Parents had a traditional faith i genuinely respected but could not replicate. A childhood riddled with the failings of incompetent guardians left me permanently ill-suited for prayer to an omnipotent caretaking authority figure. Appreciative as i am for my Parents' faith, it wasn't a good fit for me. Too much of who i am and what i've survived gets in the way.

The premise of prayer makes sense, though, if i think of the Universe as an expression of dynamic creative energy. When i find myself walking or driving underneath overhead power lines, and i hear electricity buzzing and crackling through the wires, this is how i metaphorically hear the energy that created everything that is. This energy is palpable and potent. It is abundant and infinite. It is constructive, destructive, transformative.

It made me. It is me. It is beyond me.

What i feel with this energy isn't parental, it's partnership. A relationship, to be sure, but one of alignment rather than authority.

Gratitude connects me to this energy. Prayer does, too. Gratitude comes more easily. It's my appreciation for all that tangibly is, all that has already come to be. Being warm, being in nature, being with loved ones, being at brunch – for all ways of being, i can do gratitude every minute of every hour of every day.

Prayer presents more of a challenge. It's unverifiable. It's unreliable. It demands trust.

Am i connected? Does prayer matter? There's no way to know for sure. Then there's the discomfort of setting my mouth to say something helpful when the loudest voices in my head are shouting something hurtful. It's the emotional and mental equivalent of bench-pressing twice my body weight. Sometimes, i hardly have the strength for it.

My first prayers for a Parent, in my mid-20s, were a heavy lift. Reluctant and soaked in resentment, these prayers were for a Father you haven't yet met in this story. He's the Father who stole my childhood. It felt emotionally grinding and physically taxing to pray for someone i held as contemptible, irredeemable, unworthy. But i also felt myself at the start of my adulthood held hostage by suffering and on the verge of taking my life.

Prayer was a concession then, a means to release me from a prison of emotional pain. Short, brusque, and involving choice expletives, it sounded like: "He doesn't __________ deserve this, i shouldn't have to __________ do this, but OK, may he be forgiven. Amen."

Consistently, each day for 30 days, i kept at this prayer, eventually with less swearing, always adding "amen" at the end. It's how i learned to seal a prayer, with "let it be so" resolve. And, wow, i think the "amen" worked because these ugly prayers produced an outright miracle. They changed me.

Not radically so, just enough to be willing to err on the side of love.

Meanwhile, the contemptible, irredeemable, unworthy Father who stole my childhood stumbled upon his own miracle. He found his heart at a funeral and unlocked a wholly different version of himself. That Father, redeemed by love, eventually became my Dad.

If i hadn't prayed for him in the beginning, i would've missed our miracles in the end.

Starting from the reluctant petitions i spat out for my Father, i arrived at the end of my Dad's life as the one person best-positioned to pray on his behalf. Not just because i was willing, which itself defied expectations and was unfathomable in early adulthood. But also because experience had shown me, even ugly prayers can be pretty powerful.

Once again relying on consistency, every day of his final year, i sent the same energy and request into the ether for my Dad: He doesn't harm anyone, no one harms him, and he dies safely and peacefully in his home. Amen.

On those days when the Old Soldier kicked up a conflict, like refusing to answer the door for his hospice nurse, i'd wonder if prayer mattered, or if maybe this stubborn circumstance was impervious to prayer. Then serendipity would step in, like when a trusted family friend dropped by to check on my Dad just as hospice arrived, getting the nurse in the door and talking my Dad back into his right mind.

Conflict would yield to calm, another day would dawn, and i'd once again pray that my Dad live unharmed, that he not harm anyone else (driving at night, gah!!!), and that he die safely and peacefully in his home. Amen.

/ . -. -.. /

The call from hospice came unexpectedly on the final Thursday of October 2022.

Of his 4 comorbidities, his heart disease seemed to be bringing his journey to an end. No timeline could be given, but his care manager thought i should see him for myself.

After delivering a work project Friday morning, i drove down and arrived in the early evening to find my Dad sitting at a metal patio table in his driveway. It'd been a month since i'd visited, and i wondered if i'd missed noticing how much he'd thinned. He now resembled the poorly nourished middle-ager he'd been before my Beloved Momma got ahold of him with her cooking.

An Army baseball cap shaded his gaunt face. His breathing was labored, he didn't offer to help with my luggage, and he seemed confused about whether his brother had gone out of town. But he got himself up from the patio table and followed me into the house.

Shortness of breath, weight loss and cognitive decline are telltale indications someone with heart disease is nearing the end of life. But Dad still didn't seem in any hurry to go.

Our first 48 hours, he ate his usual meals, we watched movies, and based on what i saw, i organized more in-home care, thinking he simply could do with additional help.

My travel plans originally included a Sunday drive home, but an instinct suggested otherwise. Fortunately, i heeded my senses. By mid-morning, Dad began refusing to eat or drink. He kept taking himself to the bathroom, but he couldn't get himself back to bed. Any time i'd get him back to bed, he'd get himself up and i'd find him planted someplace in the house, confused and exhausted.

It wasn't clear whether he was having a rough day or the situation was more terminal. He wouldn't lie down for more than 30 minutes. His restlessness kept me up for nearly 36 hours as i tried futilely to get him settled into the sleep he so enjoyed in retirement.

By Monday, when he hadn't eaten for nearly 2 days and his body began its trembling, i called on hospice for advice. They advised morphine. Though he moaned in pain, my Dad combated and resisted until he could no longer refuse.

Drama-prone distant relatives nowhere near the scene and with no experience of my Dad's situation supposedly accused me of trying to kill him, according to family gossip. As if i, or anyone for that matter, could prevail over this indestructible fighter.

The American South didn't kill him. Vietnam didn't kill him. Diverticulitis, diabetes, and cancer didn't kill him. Smoking with COPD didn't kill him. Death going up against my Dad was like shadows going up against the sun. Shadows don't wage war with the sun. They wait until the sun decides to go down.

Over the course of 10 hours, i administered 3 doses of morphine to my Dad, which should've rendered him unconscious. Instead, during a 5-minute window with me out of the room, Old Soldier again got himself out of bed and into the bathroom. Delirious and disoriented with no what or why driving his actions, it was as if his limbs fired on impulse and worked with a will of their own. Had i left it up to him, he likely would've died sitting on the loo wearing his pants.

It took constant vigilance and a hospital bed with railings to protect him from himself.

On Tuesday morning, hospice brought the bed, relocated him, and prescribed another round of morphine. Dad had stopped talking for the most part, and he quieted enough for me to think it safe to take a 20-minute hygiene break.

That's all the time he needed to attempt one last escape.

Morphine be damned, i returned to his room to find he'd pulled himself up by the railing and maneuvered one leg out of the hospital bed completely, but wound up with one leg stuck between its bars.

"Pop, where you goin'?"

"Go . . . go . . ."

"I know, Pop, you gotta go. You gotta stop fighting, Pop. It's time for you to go."

My Dad didn't speak again, and once i untangled his limbs and laid him back down, he slipped into sleep. Throughout the day and into early evening, family and friends visited not because i called but because they felt called. Meanwhile, i resolved to remain at his bedside for as long as it took, anticipating it could take a long while. His hospital bed abutted the foot of his regular bed, so i decamped to his room to keep watch and wait.

Just before 8:30pm that evening, i startled awake from a nap for no discernible reason.

Dad slept, the house was quiet, and i'd set an alarm to coincide with his next morphine dose. But a force sat me bolt upright without warning. Laying a hand on his belly, i felt its slight rise and fall. He was still here.

There was no sound, and i realized how odd this was, considering my Dad had sleep apnea and typically snored so loudly, he could be heard from one end of the house to the other. For several silent minutes, his belly rose and fell. And then, it simply stopped.

The Old Soldier died safely and peacefully in his home. Amen.

In the beginning, i didn't expect to have Parents i'd admire as Love Heroes and care for so deeply. In the end, through difference and difficulty, we made a family i now cherish.

Our story ends in love. It begins in forgiveness.

Breath and Prayer

- *When was the last time you took a deep breath? Or 3? If you could take 3 deep breaths with anyone, living or gone, who would it be and why?*

- *What comes alive in your brain and body at the mention of prayer? E.g. what specific meaning, imagery, associations, comfort, discomfort arises for you?*

- *What feels more natural for you, breathing with someone in distress, or praying with them? Whatever your way is, what does it say about how you show up for people when they're in pain?*

4. PAIN TALK

There are folks i know and love who might not ever find their way to forgiveness. One longtime friend who comes to mind lived a fractious relationship with their father. Both were equally obstinate, and they persistently fell out over who was more right, creating a tumultuous spin-cycle of drama the entirety of their adult lives.

From political views to personal expectations, their unmet needs remained constantly at odds. Conversations predictably escalated into argument, then devolved into attack.

The passive-aggressive kind.

These were well-regarded folks who couldn't be taken for openly hostile. Intellectual confrontation typically crescendoed into emotional separation. One or the other would cut off contact for months, time would blur the particulars, they'd reconnect, get into it about the previous unresolved debate, or some new debate, and fall out all over again.

Friends since our 30s, i'd been lending an ear to this real-life reality TV for 20-ish years. With that much history, i could see something. Even if my efforts were futile, it was time to finally say something.

Gingerly i asked: "What do you think about a different approach, like forgiveness?"

As expected, the idea hit a sore spot. My friend slapped back: "I will NEVER surrender."

The father passed away a few years later, and they buried their unfinished business. Death stopped the cycle, but didn't heal it. Their memories remained tinged with a sharp emotional charge. There had been no surrender. There would be no forgiveness.

"Luca, you don't know everything I've been through," my friend objected. It's a familiar and rightful protest. No, i don't know all of it for anyone, even the people i know well.

But you don't get to forgiveness without pain leading the way, and i know pain. Pain is the common chorus in our unique songs of suffering. Maybe once you know the pain i've been through, you'll know that you can get through your pain – and forgive all of it.

If life has shown me anything, it's that you'd be surprised at how much you can forgive.

Loops and Lessons

- *What pain loops are you in, what unfinished business are you holding – and what would it take to lay it down, even if the other person never changes?*

- *Who taught you how to deal with pain – and did they actually know how to deal with theirs?*

----

5. WARNING SHOT

None of the tales i'm about to tell are details i want to disclose.

My editor keeps insisting that i more concretely share my story. "Who or what are you forgiving?" they've probed. "You've been skirting around details. I sense trepidation in your writing, as though you are afraid to really go into depth about what happened."

The critique isn't wrong, it's spot-on, i'm afraid of exactly this.

A couple times for preceding sections, i conceded and rewrote vague bits to be more plainspoken. But i don't want to say more. My path to forgiveness is a river of trauma, and i don't want to write another trauma story.

Trauma is a wounding experience that fractures our sense of safety. Its message is that the world is fundamentally unsafe, and we are fundamentally unsafe in the world. Daily headlines, 911 call shows, podcasts about serial killers - trauma is already everywhere.

Some of you i know will be OK with reading trauma. Some folks i know even relax with trauma. "I can't sleep without murder," declared a friend of mine who goes to bed with crime shows playing on the bedroom TV. To that i say, to each their own. If murder is your medicine, that's not my business to mind.

Speaking solely for myself, i've had it with rampant trauma exposure.

Intentionally, i don't consume news from media outlets, and *The Sixth Sense* was the last scary movie i saw without forethought. Though i wonder, given the heartfulness embedded in M. Night Shyamalan's writing, does this 1999 classic really count as a horror film? Ah, a cursory internet search indicates yes, thanks to the film's disturbing supernatural element, i did indeed close out the 20th century with a touch of horror.

In my early 12-step recovery attempt to steady myself emotionally and gain a foothold on life, i had to give up reading Bret Easton Ellis, author of *American Psycho* and *Less Than Zero*. His fiction is rife with sadistic, soulless young adult characters who troubled me into a depressive funk.

A 12-stepper observantly suggested: "Maybe you oughta not read books like that." So obvious, yet 'til then, it hadn't occurred to me to stop ingesting so much trauma.

In 2023, i read *Finding Me: A Memoir* from Viola Davis about the tangles of adversity this actress unwound to win an Emmy, Grammy, Oscar, and Tony, known collectively as the EGOT awards. From 1962 to this writing in 2025, only 27 people have achieved EGOT status. Viola Davis is an exceptional human.

The stories in her Grammy-sealing audiobook of being persecuted for her dark-brown skin contributed to my coaching work with India-based adult professionals struggling with personal adversity and shame because of skin-color bias in their cultural context.

Still, as much as i learned from Viola Davis, and as much as i related through my own trauma, i hit the fast-forward arrow through her retelling of being sexually abused. Full up on her story's violent poverty and abject neglect, i had to titrate my trauma intake.

/ .-- .- .-. -. .. -. --. /

It's not that i'm a fragile flower. At least, i don't think so. My oldest and dearest friend from high school describes me as remarkably unafraid of other people's pain and fear.

When called upon, i can deliver in a crisis.

Like when a relaxing holiday weekend visit with a friend came to a traumatically abrupt end after a neighbor's boyfriend took a gun from a bedside table, stood in front of his frantic girlfriend to say, "This is your fault," then shot himself in the head as her children watched TV nearby in the living room.

This happened in a town of ~20,000 people where nothing much happens on purpose. Red and blue lights flashing in the living room windows at 10 o'clock on a Monday night alerted us to something awry next door as we brushed our teeth before bed.

Because i've lived the scene, "domestic violence" was my first thought when i walked outside and saw a woman standing on the sidewalk, recounting details to a police officer who hadn't yet gone in the house. When she said, "He shot himself," her legs collapsed beneath her, and i rushed forward to catch her before she hit the ground.

The small-town cop froze for a moment with pen and notepad in hand, caught off guard by the reveal. My friend, a marathon runner as it happens, instinctively took flight, running away in her pajamas before she could stop herself.

For several hours, i held this woman as she relived the shooting multiple times in the retelling of it: to another police officer; on the phone to the dead man's mother who screamingly repeated her son's accusation of the shooting being the girlfriend's fault; to the mental health counselor who arrived on the scene and took over crisis care.

Supporting people through hard things is a hard-earned skill i've honed over 3 decades of transforming my own trauma. It's also how i butter my bread and keep the lights on: i teach, train, and guide adult professionals through challenge and change. But unlike in my early adulthood, my personal brand is no longer crisis.

Trauma is a monster that can eat me alive. It's not a beast i can feed and stay mentally stable and well enough to develop others productively. With trauma already integral to my professional life, i can't have it also occupying my personal life.

/ .-- .- .-. -. .. -. --. /

As much as i want little-to-none of it, trauma seems integral to the human experience. There's no getting around reality. We hurt and harm each other, and we make art and entertainment out of hurt and harm. It's what we do.

When i unintentionally foisted harm on someone i loved, though, i learned a memorable lesson about the risk of sharing personal trauma without considering the impact.

In my late 20s, i unveiled a plethora of sordid details to someone i was dating because i hoped to marry her, and i wanted her to know the truth of me.

Unfortunately, what i shared sat too heavily with her. She had her own traumas, and the heaviness of mine broke her heart a bit. She said she couldn't unsee what she'd heard. She couldn't shake loose from feeling it.

This is how i came to know the experience, if not the language, of vicarious trauma.

This trauma type hadn't yet been named 30+ years ago. There wasn't widespread comprehension or common vernacular for how pain-inducing it can be to witness or hear about awful things happening to other people. We weren't explicitly aware of how visuals and words transfer the energy of injury and suffering from one body to another.

Nowadays, research and articles readily highlight adverse mental health impacts on first responders, war correspondents, healthcare professionals, teachers, and anyone whose work overloads them with chemical buildup from other people's trauma.

Even writing and reading my own stories, i sometimes needed to scrub my mind clean with a disinfecting walk in the sun afterward. Nobody needs more trauma.

That's why i ask, before you read the next section, take a minute and think it through.

If you're a highly sensitive person, or you find trauma stories overwhelming, there's no need to wade in this brackish water to get the point: We can survive horrendous crimes against our humanity, and we can forgive them.

Skip over "Monster Stories" and move on to "Stuck at the Knees" - i'll meet you there and get you re-oriented as the story winds along.

If your trauma capacity is so expansive that you can't sleep without murder, or if you need to see the trauma for yourself to believe it, OK then.

You've been warned.

Here's where it gets hard.

Aftershot

- *Consider a story you're holding close. What's keeping that story tucked away? How does it feel to keep it quiet?*

- *When have you felt someone else's pain as if it were your own? What did you do with that feeling?*

- *What's your personal sign that you've OD'd on the apocalypse for the day?*

6. MONSTER STORIES

Two young people from a middle-Alabama town meet, marry, and settle for lives on the move as military husband and wife. Their adventure takes them all the way to Germany.

Abandoned by a philandering father, he is raised by older brothers who role-model him into the Vietnam War. He is combat-wounded, tortured by nightmares of leeches and bombs, and desolate with loss. She is a survivor of a rape when she was a teenager and a subsequent abortion that stole her ability to conceive. Her temper is merciless.

They both descend from Black Africans enslaved in the American South, people who did not own their bodies. Their ancestors were stolen goods and purchased property. They were commodities utilized in service of White owners. Encoded in their DNA are notions of the body as a possession, a sexual tool, a whipping post.

Violence has been thrust upon them all their lives, reinforced by power dynamics in the racially divided South, and perpetuated through ensuing generations of family trauma.

They don't recognize individual agency or autonomy. They don't respect personal boundaries. They don't process feelings. They don't do diplomacy. They make war.

They are 26 and 24 when i come into their lives as their only child.

They are my childhood Father and Mother, and i'm pretty sure they hate each other.

Case in point, a party at an uncle's house. Kids are sequestered in a back bedroom, away from the living room, where a haze of cigarette smoke engulfs adults. The 1974 disco song "Kung Fu Fighting" blares from a stereo twice the size of a coffee table.

The song rhymes "kung fu fighting" with "fast as lightning" and "a little bit frightening."

It's insipid, but in the 1970s, it's a banger that capitalizes on the popularity of martial arts movies. The record sold around the world, from the U.S. to Australia and Europe. One of those records shakes the walls of this house party, and when i hear the words "Kung Fu," i absolutely must sneak a peek into the living room to catch the action.

My Little Kid heart is utterly in love with martial arts star Bruce Lee. In the magazines, he always looks strong. He can break a board with a 1-inch punch. He's a superman, and i yearn to be like him, with bulging arms, fast fists, and confident cool.

If the adults in the living room are doing Kung Fu, i can't miss it.

They are, and i wish i had.

Two men, my Father's brother and a friend, are each holding my Mother in place by her arms. My Father is standing atop the stereo. As i look on, my Father leaps off the stereo and karate kicks my Mother in the stomach. The men laugh, the women scream, i flee.

Moments later, my Mother fetches me from the kids' bedroom. We leave. He stays.

This happens when i'm 7. First grade had begun in the sticky hot humidity of Alabama, where my teacher had hit me with a ruler to learn my smart-talking mouth a lesson.

My Mother, a diminutive woman not much taller than 5 feet, threatened the teacher with a parking-lot beatdown and warned the principal, "Nobody hits my child but me." Partly for me, partly to keep herself out of jail, she pulled me out of the Alabama school system and refused to have me further educated in the South. Instead, we follow my Father to his Washington state duty station, and now i walk to first grade in the cold.

Luckily for my Father, this particular evening, there's a pile of fresh snow on our lawn.

Back home, my Mother sends me to my room, heads into the kitchen, and pulls a box of Cream of Wheat out of the cupboard. That's confusing. We don't eat breakfast at night. But in my room, i'm with my books, and i forget what's happening elsewhere.

Adults in my house don't read to me, i read to myself. In first grade, i'm also learning how to write, and i'm fascinated by the magical transformation that happens when a silent "e" gets added to the end of a word.

This night gives me my first memory of learning to spell a word by writing: i add a silent "e" to the end of "hop" in my notebook, elongate the O with my mouth, and magically create "hope" in the world.

The smell of Cream of Wheat brings me out of my room. All the lights are off, the whole house is dark. My Mother hears my footsteps and hollers me back into my room.

The next sound i hear is a primal howling roar, like King Kong taking gunfire. It's my Father. He stepped into the house thinking everyone was asleep and got a face full of boiling hot retaliation. Cream of Wheat coats his head. It's in his eyes, nose, ears. The snow-covered front yard saves him from complete disfigurement. He's scooping snow in his hands to smear gooey breakfast cereal off his face when the ambulance arrives.

During several weeks in bandages, he depends on his punisher for soup and tending.

Years later, when i stress-test this memory with my Mother for accuracy, i wonder why she bothered cooking Cream of Wheat when she could've simply doused him with the pot of boiling water? A Southern girl who knew a thing or two about humidity, she went with Cream of Wheat, she explained, because heat feels hotter when it sticks.

/ -- --- -. ... - . .-. ... /

My Mother is the disciplinarian. Shaped by Southern norms, her style is highest force intervention. Which is to say, she beats me with all her bodily might until i bleed. The first beating happens when i'm 8 because i kiss a girl who kisses me, and i really like it.

This girl and i live in an apartment building for military families, and we'd been playing outside in a courtyard when, the next thing i know, we're in a laundry room with the door closed. Her lips touch my lips, and my belly explodes with euphoria-butterflies.

At just that moment, her father walks in, yanking us apart mid-kiss, hollering "STOP THIS" like we're deviants committing a crime. The kiss is reported to my mother.

Before 8, i'd get a whoopin, as they say down South. Comedians cope with jokes about how whoopin's tighten up misbehaving kids. This, though, is a different level.

This beating is seared into my skin and memory by my Mother's choice of corrective instrument, the electric extension cord. For whoopin's, she employed either a belt or whatever thing happened to be in her hand when she needed to express disapproval.

But my girl-kissing deviance is so outrageous, it calls for escalated measures, and she never switches back to the belt. My Father doesn't intervene or challenge her methods.

So, from 8 to 19, i'm painfully motivated to strive for perfection or lie for protection, whichever steers me clear of her wrath. The few times a year when i fail, she brands looping U-shaped scars of varied sizes onto my arms and legs as lifelong mementos.

Perfection's purpose isn't to merit her love. No amount of perfection changes things. Straight As and exceptional achievements create no lasting goodwill. Perfection, and lying to maintain the facade of perfection, are tactics to minimize my exposure to her rage and keep me out of her lethal line of sight.

She doesn't talk so much as snaps and barks at me. When she's had too much to drink, she tells me her trauma-monster stories. Like, her father running with her in his arms, and watching over his bouncing shoulder as her mother chased after him for stealing her oldest child away. Or her mother marrying, and remarrying, and violently battling each new husband. Or the rape and infertility, and how my rage-filled Mother considered joining a convent to marry and be protected by Jesus.

Grown-ups shouldn't confide their horrors to a child, but she needs someone to listen. Since we know nothing of therapy, there's no reality in which she receives healing help.

Aside from her emotionally overloading and inappropriate reveals, we aren't close, and i don't confide in her. No more than 5 family pictures from my babyhood until my early 30s - when she dies at 57 of brain, lung, and lymph node cancer - show her holding or hugging me. We have no emotional bond, no heart-based connection.

She feeds me, clothes me, gives me books. She doesn't celebrate, encourage or praise me. She isn't someone i trust to protect or care about me. Innately, i know she doesn't love me. She's supposed to be my Mother, i do want her to love me, but she doesn't, and i can't figure out why. None of this is an idea i can verbalize. It's a reality i absorb.

Her final physical outburst against me happens when, at 19, i audaciously suggest that berating me about having lost my wallet somewhere in the house won't help me to find it. She's holding a cup of hot tea in a mug i gifted her for Mother's Day. Incensed, she rears back and hurls the full mug at me in response. Her aim is off. She's not as deadly with projectile crockery. But her violence is absurd, and pathetic, and i've had enough.

Slowly, i pick up the mug, place it on the kitchen counter, and decide we're done. So much antipathy is roiling in me, i'm starting to wish that she get cancer, suffer, and die.

College is financially out of reach. Military enlistment is my only viable option.

It's not the best idea, given how much i already can't stand authority, but i'm not running toward a future, i'm running away from the present.

As long as no one beats me, it'll be better than this.

/ -- --- -. ... - . .-. ... /

Like an old home movie on worn-out film, the images are blurred and faded, but my 8-year-old mind's eye captures the experience well enough to corroborate my body's damage testimony. The scene opens on my Father from behind, large and shadowy, walking a few steps ahead down the unlit hallway between my only-kid bedroom and the grown-up bedroom.

My only-kid room safekeeps all my favorite things: my chronologically organized stack of *Archie* comics for amusement; my facts-packed volumes of *Encyclopedia Britannica* for amazement; my radio tuned to *Dick Clark's American Top 40 Countdown*. Television doesn't yet exist for me. Books and music are my portals to the world.

Because the military-owned apartment we occupy is subject to surprise inspections, our place is maintained with pristine cleanliness. The living room is solely for visitors, the dining room is solely for meals, and i don't go into the kitchen without permission. Nowhere in this home feels like my home except the space i call my room.

The grown-up bedroom is strictly off-limits to me. Even on weekly cleaning days, when i dust every knick-knack in the apartment, i obediently stay out of this room.

Just one time, i snuck in to rummage the closet in search of Christmas presents. Older kids at school were spreading misinformation that Santa Claus wasn't real. They said if i looked for presents in the grown-up bedroom, i'd find the evidence for myself.

No presents. Lots of magazines. All with pictures of women. None of the women wore any clothes. All of them spread their legs very wide. They all smiled, but it still felt icky to look at them, the same as it felt that time i saw a dead body in a casket at a funeral.

Santa was still alive. The naked bodies were icky and dead.

Home alone with my Father as we head toward the grown-up room, i feel icky again.

Something is wrong, i don't know what, and i don't question, i don't protest, i don't resist. My 8-year-old memory doesn't retain how i came to be following behind my Father; i imagine he must've summoned me out of my room, and i quietly complied.

The bed in the grown-up room sits higher than mine. My legs dangle over the side when i lie back, naked below my belly. The pictures in the closet tell me what i'm supposed to do with my legs.

This is a silent home movie. There's no recorded memory of sound. No instructions, no voices, cars, or neighbors. No barking dogs. Not even the sound of my own breathing.

Punishment scars from my first kiss haven't fully healed, and my Father is touching me. This time, no adult appears to put a stop to what's happening. This time, no butterflies.

A tingling sensation floods my small body and overwhelms my tender nervous system.

As i get older and hear the word "pleasure" in pop culture, my body recalls (and recoils at) this sensual flood. My body associates pleasure with poison.

And, therapy be damned, i still feel about "pleasure" as a concept the way Millennials feel about "moist" as a word. It's gross, salacious. Nothing feels right about pleasure.

At 8 years old, my childhood is effectively over. Like the naked bodies in the magazine pictures, my childhood is now icky and dead. This violation awakens my sexuality and kills my innocence. It is an original sin against my body.

My Mother hardened my childhood, but my Father ended it. That's why my forgiveness journey had to start with him. What he did made way for so much more harm to follow.

My Mother's violence and my Father's violation extend their family histories of the body as a possession, a sexual tool, a whipping post.

For now, my vulnerable body belongs to them, not to the person inside.

But someday, i hope, i'll get to make my own family, and this mother and father who hurt me, they won't be my parents.

/ -- --- -. ... - . .-. ... /

Candid Polaroid snapshots from my childhood are littered with beer cans and liquor bottles in the foreground. Glassy-eyed grown-ups with jobs, kids and responsibilities hold on to each other to keep one or more standing long enough for a flashbulb to pop.

Photos from my baby christening strike me not for the sanctity of the occasion but for the beer brands on display at the after-party.

In a band of dangerously drunk adults, my Father is worst among them. Full up with alcohol and instability, he's best when absent. At home, he's never not intoxicated.

He teaches me to ride a bicycle when i'm 7 by drunkenly slow-driving a car behind me, shouting instructions as the two of us teeter and swerve down a neighborhood road.

Just as i get the hang of balancing while pedaling, my Father nosedives the car into a ditch. My first bike ride becomes me getting my 7-year-old self home to report that my Father has fallen into a hole. Police are arresting him by the time we get back to the car.

My Father is not my hero. When i'm 9, i find out he's not even my Father.

On Christmas Day, after i'd opened presents that could only have come from Santa, my Mother sits me down to tell me that i'm adopted and my "real" mother is German.

My Father is passed-out drunk on the couch, uninvolved in the moment. No mention is made of my "real" father. Putting the pieces together from what i'm hearing, though, it seems reasonable in my 9-year-old mind to presume, whoever he is, it's not this guy.

The revelation doesn't alter my immediate circumstances, but it's still a help to know these people aren't my parents, and who they are isn't my fault. What baffles me into my 20s, what i definitely can't make out as a kid, is why they would choose me if the best they were gonna do is misuse me.

On the school bus some time after Christmas break, when a schoolmate inquires why my Mother is chocolate brown, and i'm milky brown, i announce my interesting fact.

News gets around, and a neighborhood parent drops by to discuss. Out of curiosity? Or concern? Or to gossip? It's a mystery to me still.

All i know is when their visit ends, my Mother bursts into my bedroom, enraged at this invasion of her privacy. She hasn't divulged her backstory of rape, abortion and infertility, but the reminder of its existence inflames her with shame.

Ever since i could talk, she rants, i've had too damn much to say. How dare i let family business out the front door? To shut my mouth, she commands that i strip and stand barefoot and naked in a corner of my room until she says i can move. If i need to pee, hold it. Do not pee on her floor. My task is to think about how everything in my room has come from her because my "real" mother didn't want me. "*I* am your mother," she thunders, "and I betta not hear you say otherwise, or I will beat the breath outta you."

Emotional terrorism is a brutalizing reaction to a kid caught in the tangled mess of adult relationships. Her viciousness ignites an equally fierce reaction in me. Naked and cold on the outside, i feel a burning anger inside. Defying her orders, i think for myself: You are NOT my mother, and when I grow up, i will never need you or anyone ever again.

/ -- --- -. ... - . .-. ... /

Much to my relief, my war-making Mother and Father divorce just as i start middle school. Now i only have to survive one of them. The Army ships my Father to Korea, and i head to the Midwest with my Mother who moves us in with one of her brothers.

Seven of us cram into a 2-story, 2-bedroom roach-infested apartment. My uncle and aunt have their bedroom. The kids – me at 13, my 3 cousins at 10, 7 and 3 – share a room and sleep 2 apiece on bunk beds. My Mother sleeps on a living room couch with a sagging dip in the middle.

My uncle is larger, stronger, and meaner than my Mother. He loves his gleaming black 1979 Dodge Charger, and not much else. His wife is a caretaking soul. She loves her husband. She dotes on her sons. She's a nurse for premature babies. She's a healer. She doesn't hit her children. She doesn't fight her husband. She placates and pardons.

The day my Mother's brother knocks his loving wife down the stairs, my Mother packs our 3 suitcases and walks us to a motel. What i witness crystallizes my condemnation of forgiveness, compassion, vulnerability. They're all weaknesses. They'll get you killed.

Eventually, my Mother relocates us to my Grandfather's house, but first, she attempts suicide. One of our motel nights, she swallows a bottle of pills, aiming not to wake up. The label-less bottle was at the bedside; i noticed it when i shook her awake the next morning to ask if we had $2 for a fast-food breakfast from McDonald's.

Her eyes opened, and i remember their look, wide and stunned. Her first words were: "How am I still here?" In her younger years, like my Father, she was too tough to die.

If she could've, she would've left me in that motel room on my own. She doesn't beat me for waking her up. She doesn't thank me either. If she wanted to relieve herself of responsibility, she could've sent me to be raised by my Father's relatives. But they still live in Alabama, and she despises him and the South too much to hand me over.

She and i are stuck with each other. She can't leave, and there's nowhere for me to go. Without each other, we both have no one. We're dysfunctionally interdependent. We're trauma-bonded: i fear her, i'm not safe with her, but i am safe from my Father, and i'm marginally safer from the world. If my choices for now are nothing or her, i choose her.

The Grandfather who takes us in when i'm 13 hosted me the summer before i turned 12. He lived on his own in a three-story house with 3 bedrooms and a basement. So much space! Excitedly, i looked forward to peace and quiet and my own room. But throughout my stay, he brought me to his bed and touched me wherever he wanted.

Experience with my Father told me this is what men do. Experience with my Mother told me to keep this to myself.

With my Mother around, my Grandfather is distant. He leaves his own house when i'm home without her. Unable to bring me to bed, he wants nothing much to do with me. His brother, however, meets me for the first time when i'm 13, and is keenly interested.

He slips me his phone number, in case i need company.

My Mother's high school education and low skills result in work with an early-morning clock-in and a late-evening clock-out. A bus gets me to and from school, and i'm not allowed to be anywhere else other than home. Starved for attention, i dial the number, and in 15 minutes, a wrinkled old man is sitting on the couch with his trousers undone.

By now, i know what men in the family want from me. If i give it to them, i get their love. Disgusted by the arrangement, ashamed at what i've invited, i summon the will to reject this eager old molester's invitation. He can shove his love back in his pants and go.

/ -- --- -. ... - . .-. ... /

In the first half of ninth grade, just after i turn 14, my Mother and my Father announce their plans to remarry, and i feel the ceiling collapse on my life.

My Grandfather wants his house back, and my Mother needs a means to survive. A man with a government job is a means. As much as i hate her pragmatism, i can't be mad at it, and even low-key respect it.

So i accommodatingly lay my lanky frame behind the front seats of my Father's Nissan 280ZX two-seater sports car and ride in a cramped position for a week as he relocates us from the Midwest to his current duty station in the Southwest. At gas station stops, i discover that if i deeply inhale fuel fumes, they put my uncomfortable body to sleep.

Once we arrive, i drop into the last half ninth grade at a new school with kids who've known each other since kindergarten. With no friends and no desire to be at home, i spend my free time riding my bike and playing kickball, putting my foot into the ball as hard as i can to see if i can tear a hole through it.

By 14 years old, i am overrun with rage, and with so much i'll need to forgive.

/ -- --- -. ... - . .-. ... /

"Why are you so mad? What are you so angry about? Why are you so difficult?"

From high school well into adulthood, i get these questions a lot. Always rhetorical, though. It's a thing people do. We ask questions in the heat of an emotional moment, not to draw out clarity, but to express our consternation. Since the question isn't really a question, it's easily overlooked as a meaningful prompt for awareness and insight.

When i find myself in my early 30s, during my first trip to the Middle East, standing on the dusty side of a two-lane road, raging at the only person who can get me back to safety, it dawns on me to find an answer for why i'm such an explosive volcano.

A Jordanian friend from college had invited me to visit his family's home in Amman during Ramadan. For a week, i lived like a local: fasting during the day; breaking fast with his Mother's love-filled cooking after sunset; and wiling away our nights at shisha cafés smoking tobacco so strong, it left me nauseously hanging out of the car window for fresh air on the rides home.

It was a phenomenal introductory visit to the region.

But the day he took me horseback riding, i kinda lost my shite. He had sorted out our taxi ride to a riding ranch on the outskirts of Amman, but once we were done, we didn't have transportation arranged to get us home.

That's how i came to be standing on the roadside, swearing uncontrollably at my friend, and generally freaking the eff out.

Calm and casual on his home turf, he threw up an arm in the universal taxi-hailing gesture and asked: "You know we're gonna be OK, right? Why are you so angry?"

Actually, i had no idea whether we were gonna be OK. That was the problem.

An obviously foreign woman standing on a roadside, what the hell was he thinking? Had he never read the news? Was he *trying* to get me kidnapped? He was a man, and he belonged here. He had no idea of the danger of being a woman, and a foreign woman at that. How dare he be so clueless and careless with my safety?

So many people had been clueless and careless with my safety. In that moment, i couldn't see him or our situation any other way.

If there's an Official List of Feelings, "hangry" should be on it, but not having eaten for hours and hours wasn't really my issue. My hunger-induced diminished capacity was why i couldn't manage myself through anger. But it wasn't what i was angry about.

The reason i was angry, the reason i was always angry, is that i felt vulnerable to threat and danger. My go-to response to any threat-level, major or minor, was anger.

Actually, it was rage.

Rage commanded people's attention, then scared them away, or yanked them in line.

Rage was how i created safety.

Rage wasn't fail-safe, and it scared off people i wanted to keep close. But when it hit an intended target, rage incinerated a threat with red-hot flamethrower effectiveness.

My Father stops touching me when he meets my rage. By 16, i'm tall enough to look him in the eye and despise him. For years, i'd stayed silent and compliant, waiting for him to stop. He didn't. He was always drunk and vile.

The final time, he acts boldly in the presence, but not in full view, of my Mother. We are all 3 piled on the floor of the TV room. As she watches TV, i feel his hand reach over her body to find and fondle mine.

If she ever knew, she never said. In any case, it doesn't matter, i need to handle this myself. Quietly, i stand up, call him into the kitchen, and step close, face-to-face.

"If you touch me again," i hiss, "I will kill you. I mean it, if you ever put your hands on me again, I will kill you in your sleep."

My Father sees in my eyes a wrath similar to the kind he's been battling in my Mother. The ferocious fighter has raised me in her image, and my time as a victim is over. There are now 2 warrior women in his household. If he tests me, there will be consequences.

For the next 2 years until i graduate high school, my Father and i coexist under mostly civil conditions. But when it becomes apparent that i've started dating boys - an empty birth control pill packet mindlessly thrown in the kitchen garbage - my Father wants me out of the house, ironically, for being sexually active.

Actually, i'm resolutely disinterested in sex with teen boys; i go out with them because i don't know yet that i want to be with girls. A boy who wouldn't take my first or second "no" for an answer is why i'm on birth control. He hears me yell in protest, but he won't heed my words. Only a physical tussle in the front seat of his car gets him to stop.

If i'd known as a teen girl how testosterone amps up drive and determination, i'd have stayed outta cars with testosterone-driven boys. Realizing date-rape is real, i truck myself to Planned Parenthood and take advantage of options my Mother didn't have.

My Father getting up in my sexual business is one of the last exchanges i have as his child. He has never acknowledged or atoned for the liberties he's taken with my body, and he no longer gets to behave like he owns me, like i belong to him. He has no right to further influence, discuss, or control my sexuality.

That's my middle-aged summary of how things ended with my childhood Father.

My emotionally limited teen-self lacks the capability to set and express boundaries with sophisticated conviction. She's also a warrior, and like the warriors who raised her, she doesn't process feelings, do diplomacy, or use thoughtful words.

What i think and feel about my Father before i cut ties is more straightforward and raw.

My rage speaks on my behalf.

"As far as i'm concerned," it says, "he can eff off and die."

Looking Back, Before We Move On

- *OK, so, what part of Monster Stories do you feel in your gut the most? Like, what hit deep or caught you off guard? No need to explain, just note and notice.*

- *As a kid, i rarely ever felt safe, especially at home. Consider yourself as a kid, where did you go – mentally or physically – when things got too hard?*

- *Rage was survival in my story, but not everyone fights with fire. What's your go-to emotion, the one you lean on to protect yourself when things get hard? What's one hard thing that emotion helped you get through?*

7. STUCK AT THE KNEES

At 19, i decide i'm grown enough to take ownership of my life. Within 5 years, i'm flailing and floundering in 12-step recovery. My tether to life feels tenuous at best.

Actually, a quick pivot here as i realize, i've mentioned 12-step a few times, but some folks might be unfamiliar with it. So here's a quick primer from my 11 years in recovery.

In the mid-1930s, as the story's told, Dr. Bob Smith and Bill Wilson, an Ohio surgeon and a New York stockbroker respectively, were introduced while each in the grip of alcoholism. Their endeavor to sober up and recover functional lives was based on a combination of (1) mutual support through shared experience and (2) behavior change driven by what they called a set of spiritual principles.

Bill and Dr. Bob's spiritual recovery principles were religion-adjacent but absent the characterization of addiction as an individual's moral failing. Their approach attended secondarily to the why of addiction, emphasizing instead the how of creating change.

Their practice became the 12 Steps, a user manual for recovery from lives in complete chaos. When you take Step 1, you admit 2 things: your life is unmanageable, and you are powerless over all the things that make your life unmanageable.

For me, recovery meant relinquishing the toxic i-can-do-it-by-myself control i tried to exert over reality. And it meant forgoing the sensory stimulations and external escapes that suppressed and distracted my demons. In the beginning, it was the worst.

My recreational substance use had little to do with fun and a lot to do with sedation. Sugar kept me pacified but never satisfied. My young-adult relationships delivered a steady supply of crises and drama. If we'd also had social media, i'da been hooked.

Recovery meant eschewing all of it and signing up to feel ALL my feelings. Far from relief, recovery initially intensified everything that plagued me. Clearly, i'd gotten my demons and me into more than we could get through, and now we were in real trouble.

This is how i came to forgiveness: as a swim-or-drown effort born out of desperation, prompted by infuriating guidance and hard truth. The whole of it started with just one question from a fellow 12-stepper, a father who had damaged his daughters the way the Father who'd stolen my childhood had damaged me.

This unnamed 12-stepper had labored for years on his recovery by the time we met in the rooms, as they say, and his 30-something adult children still hated him. He drew a grim throughline from their inability to forgive to lives undone by ongoing self-sabotage.

"What I did, they're right to never speak to me again," he told me. "They're holding pain I gave them. But as long as they hold this pain, they give me power over their lives that I shouldn't have. It's gonna kill 'em. If you don't forgive, your pain and rage will kill you, too. Figure out how to forgive, or you're gonna die. Forgive like your life depends on it."

Suicidal ideation had entrenched itself in me as a coping mechanism, so his prediction wasn't alarmist. In his chronically unwell children, he saw my past, present, and future.

He knew i'd come into 12-step to dodge self-destruction and recover an ability to live.

"You said you don't deserve forgiveness, at least you're sober in recovery," i insisted. "My Father's too drunk to be sorry. You don't forgive people who can't even be sorry."

My hardline proclamation came from a childhood of seeing forgiveness misused and manipulated by people to keep doing dirty deeds. Perpetrators didn't apologize, plead guilty, or express remorse until after they'd been caught and convicted. As i saw it, the iron fist of consequence struck harder and straightened out crooked behavior.

Forgiveness changed nothing.

The Christian churchfolk of my childhood promoted forgiveness as a divine high road that followers traveled to be more like Jesus. Hmph. How i read it, the story of Jesus exposed forgiveness as a weakness that could get you killed.

In a ruthless world, i wasn't tryna be Jesus.

"You're hearing what you wanna hear," the 12-stepper countered. "I didn't say nothing about not deserving forgiveness." A fair rebuttal, but i hard-headedly wouldn't admit it.

Then he asked me this: "If your Father was a stranger, if you didn't know him, and you were never gonna see him again, would you let him have this power over you?"

"But that's not . . ."

"What would you do? Would you let him have this power over you?"

"NO! OK, no. But i don't know what to do. How do I forgive this?"

"For 30 days, get down on your knees and pray for him," he advised. "Don't pray for *you* to forgive him. Just pray that he be forgiven."

Gotdangit, these 12-steppers were constantly directing me to do a thing for 30 days. That's a stretch of forever when you're dangling over the emotional edge.

Also, the "down on my knees" part. As if i should submit to pleasing or pleading with some Authority on high. Why hadn't It interceded when i most needed? Why didn't It shield me from the harm i now had to pray about and repair? The irony was galling.

A history of hurt so clogged my ears, i missed the liberating flexibility embedded in this 12-stepper's straightforward and simply crafted forgiveness process.

It wasn't me who had to forgive my Father, just someone or something or whatever. The only action i needed to take was to put a constructive positive declaration about him out into the ether as a kind of petition on his behalf.

But i got stuck at the "knees" and knocked fully sideways by my staunch resistance to all things religious.

/ ... ..- .-. .-. . -. -.. . .-. /

Not until well after my Beloved Momma came into my late-20s adulthood could i hear church, Lord, and love in the same sentence. My Southern Baptist upbringing and its incumbent fearsome God seemed hellbent on exploiting and damning the vulnerable.

Black gospel music was a saving grace. Thick multi-layered harmonies soothed our souls and assured with raw intensity that we'd overcome our adversities, survive our darkest night, and bask in the promise of morning.

But not even the choir could compensate for many of the church-going adults in my childhood operating inherently and unconsciously like slave-holding overseers.

They commanded unquestioned obedience.

They vilified and punished with ferocity.

They reeked of hypocrisy.

Men beat their wives, women beat their children, and everyone hid their welts and bruises beneath their Sunday best. Fire-and-brimstone sermons warned against sin and preached repentance, but also co-signed and reinforced a man's right to rule his house, a woman's duty to submit herself to that rule, and a child having no rights at all.

These elders of my childhood and the power they worshipped had no business being in charge of a human life.

So be it. If no one could look after me, i'd look after myself. Wielding resistance and defiance as weapons of self-preservation, i grew rabidly self-protective, self-reliant, self-directed, and self-determined. Inside, i was a feral cat mixed with a lone wolf.

Post-high school, my young adulthood began in my late teens with severing from the people who raised me. As soon as i could legally and financially determine my fate, i moved out of their home, got out from under their authority, fired the lot of them, and took control of my life.

Trouble, of course, showed up in short order. Severing from dysfunctional people did nothing to remedy the dysfunction ingrained in me. Wherever i went, our past followed. Effectively, i had no training and no clue how to operate as a functional adult. It's like i'd wrested control of a jumbo jet over the ocean, then realized i had no idea how to fly.

Actively spiraling and descending toward suicide in early adulthood indicated that i, too, had no business being in charge of a human life.

So it was that i signed onto 12-step recovery, where i emotionally kicked and screamed through 30-day directions from survivors who understood firsthand my type of crazy.

All of us, the violators and the violated, dragged ourselves through scarred histories as we figured out together how to live and be alive. We were varied degrees of emotionally stunted and cognitively impaired, woefully unable to cope with life on life's terms.

The somewhat capable guided the barely able. Many of us struggled to absorb sound advice through warped sensibilities, trust deficiencies, and unrelenting stubbornness.

Fortunately, i'd been able to make use of 12-step guidance to identify a power, any power, beyond myself, and release to it the chaos-making chokehold i had on my life.

My first step was to secure an advocate i could lean on for help. Other 12-steppers spoke of a Higher Power. While i couldn't resonate with belief in a higher being, my spirit did connect to the notion of a power operating alongside me because i could concretely see it at work in the serendipities that supported my fumbling will to live.

One huge bit of kismet: i didn't find recovery, it found me by way of a crack-addicted convicted felon ordered into 28-day treatment while she and i were dating. A therapist ignored his conservative peers, respected same-sex couplehood, and included me in family therapy. To my dismay, we uncovered my hard-wired craving for harm-inducing relationships, an addiction called codependency. It was my first exposure to any kind of therapy; i went in thinking "i'm not the problem" and came out an emotional wreck.

It wasn't addiction so much as rage about – and underneath – addiction that drove me to recovery. Because family therapy left me with a savage urge to put my fists through glass, i opted into group therapy at the treatment center. If the group had focused on mindfulness and meditation, maybe i'd be talking about that now. But this group did 12-step, so that's what i did. It was free, and i didn't trust what i might otherwise do.

Treatment didn't stick for the person whose addiction brought me face-to-face with my own, but i immediately went all-in. A new job far away opened an escape hatch for my fledgling recovery and me to strike out on our own in search of more life-saving grace.

A wealth of serendipities followed, chief among them was a fortuitous open-hearted connection with a man who shed his shame and admitted his shortcomings to help a damaged and defiant newcomer.

This man earned my respect and attention because he owned his failures, told the truth about himself, and held himself accountable. He had a mission in life to do something good with all the bad. He wasn't tending to his reputation, his image, his brand, or his opinion. He was focused on how to be of service.

He couldn't fix his family, but he could be of use to someone.

Through his efforts to become more than what he had done, he'd become someone i wanted to be: a person who could positively impact a life.

Then he told me to get down on my knees and pray my Father be forgiven, all of which smacked of old-time religious subjugation. My insides roared in protest.

/ ... ..- .-. .-. . -. -.. . .-. /

Submission, subjugation, surrender – these were set-ups for violation and oppression, and i wanted no part of any of it. Once i decided i had tolerated enough, there was no authority to whom i would submit.

My inability to yield cost me a career in the military after i came out to myself as gay. Before the rules changed in the 1990s, the United States government required new recruits to confirm they had no homosexual or bisexual tendencies. My recruitment file included a duly signed form because the pretty third-grade girl who kissed me when i was 8 didn't count – and nevermind that explosion of euphoria-butterflies in my belly.

The electric extension cord whipping i received to beat the queer out of me failed at its original intent but succeeded spectacularly in beating self-hate and submission into my 8-year-old body and soul.

With my tendencies forcibly suppressed, i compliantly signed the government form and headed to bootcamp after high school. The adults responsible for my future had done nothing to prepare for or put me through college. Maybe with military service, i could take care of this myself.

Then a whole other pretty woman who'd been a friend kissed me just after i turned 19, and the butterflies exploded again, plunging me into a full-on panic. Why did girls want to, like, kiss me?! Did i want them to? Why did i want them to?! It's a wildly untenable dilemma, finding out you're probably homosexual when you're already homophobic.

Also, i'd signed the freakin' form. One year into my 4-year enlistment contract, i could now be prosecuted and criminalized for tendencies i didn't know of, want or choose.

It was one thing to fight off threats from without, but this threat was within: i was the thing i hated. There was no one i could think to talk to, nowhere i knew to go for help.

For the first time in my life i thought, let's just leave.

Moving swiftly from thought to deed, i rummaged through my military roommate's medicine cabinet for a way to end my life. Nothing effective and painless was on hand, and for my first brush with suicide, i wasn't ready or prepared for messier alternatives.

Living in fear of military authority also would not stand. So, i armed myself with just enough legal guidance to avoid prosecution, skipped the requisite chain of command, and outed myself to the officer in charge of my unit. Within 6 weeks, the 2-star general of the military base where i was stationed approved my honorable discharge, and i quit.

If i could've stayed in the military, i'd be retired by now with a secure pension, a lot less student loan debt, and people regularly thanking me for my service. But i just could not hide, and i could not submit.

My rage-blind and most vulnerable parts demanded safeguarding from authority at all costs. No one was going to dictate how i lived my life, or make a mess of it, except me.

As a child who'd been abusively required to submit and surrender to authority, there was no opportunity and no good reason to distinguish between surrender, submission, and subjugation. These were all the same threat.

By early adulthood, my survival-based emotional demands were tightly wound around protection, truth, justice, retribution, and recognition that i had been so grievously and grossly mishandled as a child by the people who raised me.

What i wanted was for those who'd abused their power over me to acknowledge what they'd done and pay for it with their lives.

What i got was direction to forgive in a way that violated my survival-based contempt for any and all authority.

Justified as they were, my survival-based emotional demands weren't always my allies. They helped me endure, but they didn't represent the sanest parts of myself, and they were prone to sacrificing my future for the sake of safety.

Driven by these demands, what i didn't understand is that feelings are true, but feelings aren't facts. They're important information and useful data, but my feelings aren't facts.

This insightful distinction didn't land until my 30s when a therapist challenged me to rethink a relationship situation. Whatever a girlfriend-of-the-moment had done, i can't even recall now, it'd felt similar to behavior i'd experienced in childhood with a parent.

The therapist made a clarifying observation: "Your experience is real, and your feelings are true for you, but what happened then is not the same as what's happening now."

"Yeah," i argued, "but it feels the same."

The therapist held the line: "But they're not the same."

"Yeah, but it FEELS the same! And isn't that why i'm in here, to deal with my feelings?!" i shouted, because now i was also feeling unheard, and i learned to shout when i didn't feel heard, another insight unearthed later in my adulthood.

Unfazed by my agitation, the therapist dropped this brain bomb: "You're in here to deal with your behavior. How long will you keep behaving like your girlfriend is a parent, and you're still a child? You're an adult. Who's in charge? You, or your childhood feelings?"

My head buzzed as my worldview cracked open. The therapist earned the final word. For the rest of our session, i silently journaled about how my feelings could be doing me a disservice, retarding and calcifying my thinking, deforming and dictating reality.

My feelings didn't just reflect my experience, they defined the world for me.

Not until my 30s did i finally come to see this as a limitation to be addressed.

In the 20+ years since, shifting and maturing my relationship with my feelings has been a perennial life assignment. Just when i think i've finished all my homework and passed my finals, i stumble into a next-level limitation and learn i still got some growing to do.

/ ... ..- .-. .-. . -. -.. . .-. /

Back in my 20s, i'm at the beginning of my forgiveness journey. Quick to protest and tough to convince, i argue with fierce boldness and mad intensity. The more authority people claim to have, the more likely i am to stare them down. Power doesn't scare me, it dares me. Folks are telling me i should become a lawyer (like i got law-school money). Stand, push, fight come naturally. Accommodate, acquiesce, kneel do not.

Being told to pray when i know it's undeserved, and down on my knees at that, i can't make it make sense. Barely willing to do the praying, i'm NOT at all about to get down on my knees to do it.

"No effing way, i mean, c'mon," i balked, "is that absolutely necessary?"

"Of course, it's not necessary. Feel free to do this your way. See where that gets you."

The "feel free" got me. Of all the feelings i felt, free didn't figure among them. More than anything, i wanted to know, was it even legitimately possible for me to feel free?

If i'd had any useful answers, my life wouldn't have been so unmanageable, unlivable, and in dire need of intervention from strangers.

All i knew is what i firmly felt and believed to be true. Under siege and self-limited, i lacked the curiosity to question my feelings. Nuance also escaped me, and i needed prompts and inspiration from others to consider and comprehend the world differently.

At the heart of it, this is what i was doing in my 11 years of 12-step, training myself in new ways to perceive and engage with the world. Recovery didn't cure my rage, but it did help me expand my emotional range enough to interact with the world in different ways. This self-development helped me become a more functional human being.

A world-weary misanthrope lives in me still and refuses to this day to follow social rules without questioning where they've come from and what underlying purpose they serve.

But fortunately in my early 20s, i came across a quote from poet Maya Angelou that kept me from fully devolving into an insufferably bitter adult. This Civil Rights activist and all-around beacon of light called a cynical young person "one of the saddest things in the world" because they've "gone from knowing nothing to believing nothing." It put me on notice about living a life where all i knew were the broken experiences i'd had.

/ ... ..- .-. .-. . -. -.. . .-. /

Much of my growth in 12-step came from learning to comprehend words differently.

Listening to and challenged by 12-steppers, i journaled voraciously to capture when anyone used a word in a way that expanded my thinking and reframed my possibilities.

In notebooks i carried, on paper scraps when i didn't have a notebook, on paper-towel sheets when i couldn't find scraps of paper, i filled myself with ideas about how words could mean more than what i'd experienced them to mean.

Forgiveness was one of those words. Surrender was another.

The whole of early recovery for me was an immersive crash course in surrender: giving up, admitting defeat, accepting powerlessness.

Surrender became the great paradox: i gain power by accepting my powerlessness; i find control by admitting i've lost control; i step into self-sustaining strength when i concede my shortcomings and ask for help.

Early recovery confronted me with the challenge to surrender my always-on guard and relax my vigilance against anyone ever having authority and power over me ever again.

Protest was such a survival reflex for me, it's doubtful i'd have thought to or been able to probe surrender outside of 12-step or solely as an intellectual exercise.

My change of heart about surrender couldn't take hold in my resistant brain without first taking root in my primal body.

/ ... ..- .-. .-. . -. -.. . .-. /

In the months after family therapy, as i fought off putting my fists through glass to be rid of addiction, another i-can't-live-like-this panic crashed into me.

Home alone in my studio apartment, i collapsed onto the floor in a heap, pressed myself to the carpet from forehead to shins, and begged "please, please, please, i can't, i can't . . . i don't wanna live like this anymore. Please, make it stop."

Don't ask me who i was imploring because i don't know myself.

As it happened, i'd thought it was an OK idea to let my crack-addicted former-felon recently-released-from-treatment girlfriend use my car to pick up dinner, and i didn't see her or my car again for 14 hours. My panic followed a night of pacing the floor, vacillating between terror that she might be dead and rage that she might be alive.

At some point, i just couldn't breathe anymore.

My emergency call out into the Universe, that was a prayer, but i didn't know it. This isn't something i'd known to do. These weren't words i'd known to say. My brain didn't determine this course of action, my body did.

Because i could no longer do the chaos, or manage my mess, or bear my burdens, or battle to live, panic in my body pummeled me into full-on face-down acquiescence.

Nope, i didn't know nothing about yoga, and i'd never heard of child's pose. Yet there i was, intuitively using my whole body to ground my wildly dysregulated nervous system. Emotional overwhelm subsided as i pleaded for help to ease the load. Breath found its way back into my body. My system calmed itself. The panic passed.

It was a moment of total surrender.

In the quiet after the storm, i pushed myself up off the floor and stood firmly on my feet. Whatever just happened, i didn't yet have words for, but i could feel i wasn't the same, and it was time to move on. With or without my car.

In hindsight, i recognize this moment as my body internalizing a distinctly different experience of surrender. Having already internalized so much forced submission and subjugation, my body now had a fresh bit of comparative data to parse the differences.

In my body i could discern the key elements of submission and subjugation: imposing force and a disempowering intent. In my body, i could identify and name the primary purpose of submission and subjugation: to dominate me, and rob me of my power.

Surrender also sometimes involved outside forces - think warring factions, rival gangs. But my face-down moment unveiled a new facet of surrender. My body experienced surrender as a power i could choose on my own terms and use for my own benefit.

Surrender was a decision i could come to for my own reasons.

When the cost of persisting on the path of chaos was too high, when the risk of doing battle with reality wasn't worth the price i might pay, i could lay down arms and let go.

For the first time, surrender became actively associated in my body with release, but it still challenged and infuriated me mentally to need surrender.

What if i couldn't figure things out on my own because i was weak, or incompetent, or useless, or the myriad other shame-based charges i levied against myself?

Actually then, all the more reason to exercise the option to surrender.

If i'm failing at life because i'm a failure, more reps of me running things weren't likely gonna improve my chances of getting from crazy to sane. But if i allowed the worst characterizations of myself to be true, then i could reasonably expect anyone as inept as me to need all the surrender and support they could get their hands on.

To this end, one of the best steps i took for my life involved admitting my crippling defeat at life. No more excuses, no more blame, no more bowing to my shame.

The problem in early recovery was that i had to admit defeat, like, ALL the time. Which meant learning the lesson of surrender repeatedly. These lessons became some of my best reps at life: i developed an emotional ability to appreciate surrender's power, the emotional buy-in to incorporate surrender into my life, and the emotional fortitude to practice surrender in the face of monumental loss, uncertainty, and fear.

These reps also taxed and pushed me harder than i thought i could stand. Like, i can't imagine how i woulda done forgiveness if i hadn't been able to cuss and fuss about it.

Upgrading my survival tactics called for an expletive-laden, embodied understanding that surrender wasn't condoning power over me, it was developing power within me.

Life in 12-step enforced and reinforced this new body-based association between surrender and self-empowerment. The forgiveness assignment put before me by my fellow 12-stepper offered yet another opportunity to upgrade.

"Go ahead," he baited, "feel free."

Surrender had already moved my life further along than i could have imagine. Here i was refusing to get down on my knees when i'd already been flat on the floor, had managed to stand again, and as a result, had set myself on the road to recovery.

If there was more to surrender than i knew, maybe there was more to forgiveness, too.

Amidst my self-righteous ranting about how i shouldn't have to do this, the wisdom in my body whispered a hard truth: "This is the way, and you know it." If i could surrender, maybe i could get to forgiveness, and maybe i really could feel free.

How i finally finagled my way around my protest-everything survival instinct: i dropped the "pro" and kept the "test". Bargaining with myself, i made a deal to test-drive and tolerate the 4-week assignment as-is, and *when* this didn't work – because, i mean, obviously – i could drop it and not waste any more of the time i couldn't afford to lose.

Moving through the 30-day task, i felt myself caught up in a kind of benevolent loop:

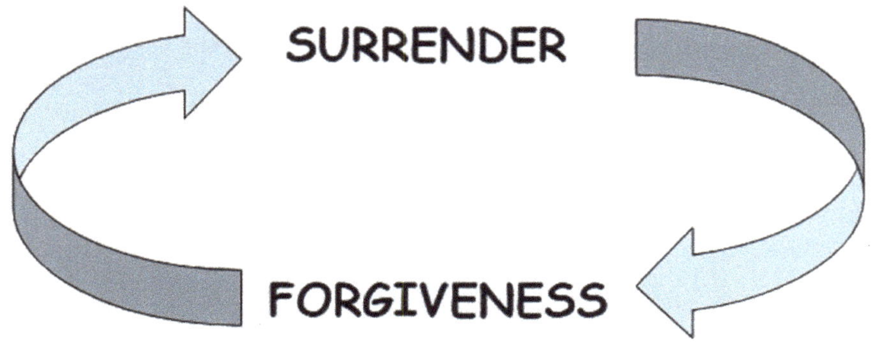

Surrender released me just enough to attempt forgiveness. Forgiveness freed me just enough to trust surrender.

If i could've continued to run my life on rampant self-control without it devolving into chaos, i would've had no impetus to change my mind, and i probably wouldn't have bothered with the heavy lift of forgiveness.

But i couldn't stay alive and in my life without changing how i lived. So, i surrendered. Despite my suspicions and defiance, i chose release over resistance. While struggling with my unbending brain, i chose to kneel and practice forgiveness with my able body.

Every day that i gave myself over to praying for my Father to be forgiven by something Out There other than me, i felt forgiveness become more directly accessible to me.

My system shifted from the inside. There was less resistance, less fight in me. There was less of an emotional demand to rage about wrongs and thrash against the past.

My Father's failings remained unacceptable, but as i occupied myself with requests that he be forgiven, i found myself less preoccupied with plans for retribution.

My heart didn't exactly fill with love, but i was also no longer hellbent on destruction.

Forgiveness astonishingly, tangibly, and positively changed everything.

Not for my Father. For me.

Forgiveness stoked my power within. It transferred decisions about how i would live with my pain out of my Father's hands and into mine. It wasn't up to him to heal me.

His acknowledgment or apology became less and less necessary.

My feelings about him stopped haunting me and defining my world. My pain stopped owning me, i didn't need to keep hurting myself and wrecking my life because of it.

Surrender released me to forgive. Forgiveness released me to surrender.

A benevolent loop of letting go, this is what set me free.

Small Words, Big Thoughts

- *What reaction does your body have to forgiveness and surrender? What do you feel? Where do you feel it? What does your brain say? What do you hear inside?*

- *If forgiveness had a personality, how would you describe it? Would it be weak? Or strong? Familiar? Or foreign? An optimist, a pessimist, or a realist? A moral thing, a healing thing, or something else entirely?*

- *Whatever lives in you about forgiveness, where did it come from? How did it get there? Where did you learn what you know and feel about forgiveness? What made those voices and knowledge sources credible or believable for you?*

---

8. ONE MORE TRY

My Mother and Father are in the thick of their second divorce when they each fall into new love relationships that will lead to forever-after marriages. As their lives take their monumental turns, i am nowhere to be found.

Elbows-deep in recovery, i go 5 years without seeing my Father and most of 7 years without seeing my Mother. Raised to honor my parents, i need time to honor myself.

The distance works like a detoxing cleanse. With them no longer trauma-vomiting on my life, i start to flush out the toxicity corroding my nervous system, oozing from my pores, afflicting me with acne, eczema, and painful periods, sinking me in depression.

Whatever the unwell adults are doing, i don't care. The best i've been able to manage is to stop wishing them dead. Then my Father nearly dies, and a cousin who's plugged into all the family goings-on extends a tentative invitation.

This is one of my favorite cousins who'd later join my Parents and me in Las Vegas for our final Thanksgiving. She's one of the few people in the family whom i trust to have my back, to look out for my well-being, to not be careless with my safety.

She lets me know my Father has almost died. She says she doesn't know if i want to call, but if i do, i can reach him at the number she provides.

A year before, i'd kicked and screamed my way into praying for him after a 12-stepper who'd committed his type of crimes challenged me to be free from my hate and rage.

The ugly prayers of my forgiveness practice have released me just enough to reach out.

In many storytellings, a phone call changes everything. In this telling, the phone call only happens because everything had already begun to change.

/ -.-. .... .- -. --. . /

Decades before she comes to be my Beloved Momma, she's the lady who answers the phone in my Father's hospital room. She's not at all what i expect when i call.

At first, i think she's a nurse – they're professionally trained to be pleasant to everyone. But she greets me like she knows me, like we're long-lost relations. When i say my name, she responds with genuine warmth, "Oh it's so GOOD to hear your voice!"

Whoever she was, it was odd to hear her voice. Here i'd called the hospital ready for the sound of a weak and dying stranger, and i got a voice wrapping me in an embrace. She went on and on about how glad she was i'd called, how glad my Daddy would be that i'd called, how she couldn't wait to meet me, how she'd seen pictures of me and "you look just like yo' Daddy. Lawdhavemercy!"

When delighted, and she was often delighted, she'd punctuate her sentences with a quintessential Southern church lady "lawdhavemercy" exclamation. It's endearing, but i'm initially unmoved. Her enthusiasm makes no sense to me, and i'm having none of it.

In case you skipped *Monster Stories*, my childhood Mother and Father informed me when i was 9 that they adopted me as a baby, and that my "real" mother was German.

"It's interesting that i look like him," i say about my Father, "seein' as how i'm adopted."

Our introduction ends abruptly. "Lemme let you talk to yo' Daddy," she demurs.

Before passing the phone on, she tells me that she loves me, and i don't reply because i'm guarded and gobsmacked: "Did this lady just tell me she loves me? Why?!"

No woman associated with my Father has ever spoken to me like this.

It'll take a while of learning to love my Parents and learning to be loved by them for me to realize, the warm acceptance i hear in her voice is the sound of unconditional love.

Though i can't yet name it, i know i want more of it.

Like recovery, i'm hooked immediately.

Also like recovery, i'm resistant and untrusting. It takes a minute to come around.

Contentedly uninvolved in my Father's life, i'm unaware of and don't participate in their Vegas nuptials following his hospital release. Their wedding photos show just 4 people in attendance: my Father's closest brother and sister-in-law, the bride, and the groom.

These photos, featured on my Parents' living room walls during their 25 years together, are memorable both for what's present, and what's missing. A broad smile anchors the whole bottom half of my Father's face. His eyes gleam. He looks deliriously happy, like he's having the time of his life. Notably, there's not a beer can or a liquor bottle in sight.

My Father didn't invite me to his wedding, and i totally get why. It's not an occasion i likely would've celebrated. In my second conversation with the woman who answered the phone, it's less of a conversation, more of an inquisition.

"What are your intentions with my Father?" i demand to know. Not because he needs my protection, but because she might. She chuckles at my unfiltered directness.

"Yo' Daddy told me you like to get to the point and say what's on yo' mind," she says, then she speaks to my question.

"I knew yo' Daddy before you was born. I intend to love him, and care for him, and be his wife, like i shoulda done from the beginning."

Hmm, so she loves him. And she sounds, like, happy about it. She, actually loves him.

What i'd known of my Father, he didn't merit this kind of goodness. But she knew him first. Maybe she knew something in him that i'd never seen. A negotiation opens in me, an opportunity to drop the "pro" and keep the "test" even though i don't trust him and i'm not pro (i.e. in favor of) him. But if she loves him, and she's a loving person, then i'll set aside my protest, play along from a distance, and see what happens.

For the next couple of years, i call sporadically, always speaking to her first. We don't talk about much of consequence. We just connect. She tells me what's growing in her garden, i tell her what i've done that day. We hit on something funny, and her laughter warms me to the core. The soothing glow in the center of my being pulls me to her.

Especially on an emotionally gray day, i call, less to talk, more to feel her love me.

When she passes me on to my Father, he asks me about the weather, and what i've eaten, and i ask him the same. Through these simple exchanges, we find civil ground.

If i don't talk to her, i don't talk to him. For right now, she's the best thing about him.

/ -.-. .... .- -. --. . /

My Mother's new fella is an old family friend, which pisses my Father off to no end. Fifteen years after the fact, when i mentioned how fortunate everyone had been to find love later in life, he still huffed about the two of them with "how dare they" indignation.

Maybe it was a man-code thing, but he just could not let those bygones be bygones. He went to his grave with their marriage on his heart as an unforgivable offense.

The two men had been stationed together in the Southwest. He'd known my Father since before i was in high school. Retired from the Army, he took up a second career teaching leadership and life skills to teens as part of Junior Reserve Officers' Training Corps programs. He volunteered to teach me how to drive, and his patient instruction helped me pass my driver's test at 16, when my Father lost his license to drunk-driving.

He was responsible and comfortable to be around like my Father had never been. He didn't drink much or smoke at all. He didn't compliment me inappropriately or objectify my body. Around him, i never felt uneasy or hypervigilant.

More than that, he felt genuinely interested in my well-being. He offered kind attention, and expected nothing in return. He was my first experience of someone behaving with me like a functional father. He was my first up-close experience of a good Dad.

He'd been around long enough to see inside our family, and he knew the marriage my Father and Mother had made. Divorced with 3 daughters and a son, all 5 to 10 years older than me, he'd also made mistakes. With all of that, he wanted to marry again.

He'd grown up serving as a protective and caretaking son to his mother. He wanted someone who needed his protection and care as a husband. After my Mother's second separation from my Father, he stepped in with emotional support and helpful hands to fix broken things around the house. Eventually, he stepped into trying to fix my Mother.

Absent during her second divorce and remarriage, i get word through family gossip channels that she's married a man i remember as good-hearted.

He's literally tall, dark and handsome with a gentle and affable way. In stark contrast to my Mother, he doesn't fuss or cuss. He withstands her tirades with the rock-steady bearing of a monk.

In their wedding photo, my Mother wears a timeless white dress and turns toward him. He has her wrapped in one arm and wears his medal-decorated military dress uniform. She calls him her knight in shining armor. Because i respect him, i call him my Stepdad.

His steady presence and their marriage lead me to wonder if things can be different between my Mother and me. Is it possible, with him, she can be good-hearted, too?

A high school teaching job for my Stepdad brings them both to California, where i'd tumbled into my 20s after quitting the military. My Mother and i hadn't been in touch, but we knew how to reach each other. When she rings, i relent, and we reconnect.

It's meaningful, and it doesn't last long.

For a brief stint in my second year of recovery, i rent a spare bedroom in their 2-story townhome - an adult arrangement my Mother and i can abide. My Stepdad proves as good-hearted as i remember, and his effect on my Mother is a marvel. In some ways, she's unrecognizable. She jokes. They laugh. She sings. They dance.

She didn't joke or laugh or sing or dance when i was a kid. She's someone i've never seen, someone i didn't know existed.

She finally has the marriage she wanted, not to Jesus, but to a man who truly loves her. She doesn't need to work. She doesn't need to struggle. She only needs to be happy.

And for a while, she is. But she can't sustain it. Her trauma monsters won't let her.

She takes up day-drinking, short bottomless glasses of brandy that never run dry.

It breaks my heart to watch my Mother drink. No matter how much my Stepdad loves her, it isn't enough to satiate the thirsty trauma monsters drowning her from the inside.

She tries once to attend 12-step with me: i walk into the room to grab seats and don't notice she's not behind me until a 12-stepper points and asks: "Is that your friend?"

"No, Dude," i say, "that's my Mom." She's standing at the threshold, unable to cross over. She sees her seat is saved. The choice is hers. She leaves and waits in the car.

Soaked and softened in brandy, my Mother is less of a menace. She's in the grip of menopausal hot flashes, so she hollers if my Stepdad dials the air-conditioning down because his fingers are blue with cold. Otherwise, she's not throwing things at me or ranting with regularity, so it's not impossible to be around her. But it is still difficult.

Mainly because she just cannot leave me alone about being gay.

A huge, and i do mean huge, part of my recovery involved accepting my sexuality and untangling from the shame-based homophobia that nearly strangled the life out of me.

If i think of sexuality as a spectrum bound by "completely heterosexual" at one end and "completely homosexual" at the other, my experience tells me many more people move about the middle than are willing to admit it.

In recovery, i stopped being one of those people unwilling to admit it. Queer folks talk about being in the closet as a euphemism for being in denial or in hiding from oneself and the world. It's isolating and debilitating in the closet. People die in there.

Liberated by recovery, i didn't just come out of the closet, i burned my closet to the ground. Personally and professionally, i fully committed to being me. Participating in pride parades and sporting a pink triangle (look it up ▼) affirmed my existence and made me visible to myself. Once i came out, there was no going back.

Recovery taught me to cope with life on life's terms. It's probably why i'm a realist. My proverbial glass of water isn't half-full or half-empty. It's just half a glass of water, and we make of it what we will.

As a realist, it's unreasonable and kinda ridiculous to expect my Mother will shift from beating homophobia into me with an extension cord to cheering my outness and pride.

Especially now that she constantly drinks, the emotional Berlin Wall i've maintained between my family and my life is as warranted as it's ever been. Zero girlfriends or friends are invited to my family home. My Mother has no view into who i care about.

Nothing about me is in her face. The bar for a decent relationship is as low as it can go.

My motto is simple: Live and let live. Agree to disagree. You do you. Let me be me.

My Mother doesn't need to embrace, accept or support me. My only ask is that she stop evangelically trying to convince me that something is wrong with me and that i should be someone other than who i am.

In no small part, i imagine, this is how she feels about herself.

"I just don't understand, and I can't change," she admits in a confessional moment.

If we can't change, we can't grow. It's an axiom i'm learning in my 20s partly through experience of a Mother who is calcified in her rigidity, and hurting herself and others.

"I don't expect you to understand being gay - you're not gay," i tell her. "Like how men from Mars and women from Venus getting together makes no sense to me - because I'm not straight. But just because we don't understand somethin' don't make it wrong. It just makes us different."

Only one of us is willing to let our differences lie.

My sexuality persists as a splinter between us. Her low-grade hostility wears me down. Having already given up on mutual love, i'm now giving up on mutual respect.

When she isn't harassing me about my sexuality, she drifts into the past and wanders around its tribulations. When she's feeling particularly prickly, she needles me with "You're just like your Father," an accusation she levied against me when i was a kid.

The association appalled me as a child, knowing my Father as i did. What she meant exactly was never clear. Her harsh tone told me she didn't think it to be a good thing.

On that point, she and i were of the same mind.

Listening with adult ears, i finally hear past the insult and catch on to the contradiction. It's a hint, i realize, she's been dropping all my life. "I'm like my Father?" i ask. "You've said this since I was a kid. How am I like my Father when you told me I'm adopted?"

She doesn't expect the inquiry, and she doesn't offer much of an answer.

"You're gonna need to go talk to him about that," is all she'll say.

Her bitterness-driven drinking strains our tenuous tie. It's like her and my Father have switched places. He's pulling himself out of the barrel, and she's rolling herself into it.

The man who'd been a drunk all his life finds his footing.

The woman who'd raged all her life slides into an alcoholic abyss.

Her violence drove me away as a teen. Her drinking shuts the door between us as adults. Ensuring my Stepdad can reach me when the time comes, i leave their home and don't see her again until 5 years later, when she's suffering and dying from cancer.

Lines Crossed, Hearts Opened

- *What's your sign that you've reached your limit with a difficult situation or person? And what do you do next?*

- *What unexpected connections or people have surprised you with kindness when you least expected it?*

9. TRUTH, AND RECONCILIATION

Between the adoption and second marriages, i'm amassing a growing collection of parental units to keep organized in my head, heart, and conversations.

My "real" mother is less a person to me, more of an idea, so her "m" stays lowercase.

My childhood Mother and Father didn't earn their titles, but it's who they formally are to me, so they get proper capitalization.

Both their spouses reparent me with an unconditional goodness that merits honorable designation. Thus, my Mother's husband becomes my Stepdad, and my Father's wife becomes my Stepmomma.

My organizing labels are intended to show and bestow respect where it's due.

But the "step" in "Stepmomma" rubs my Stepmomma the wrong way. She insists i'm her daughter, and wants me to call her Mom. Everyone calls her Mom, but i'm an only child who's already had 2 moms. Neither worked out, and i don't want another one, i tell her, as i go my own way on this. For now, she's gonna need a different label.

My inner realist prefers factual clarity, so in the early days of our relationship, before i love her with all my soul, i stick with Stepmomma.

My Stepmomma is angling for me to come visit. She promises i can have my own pie and claims sweet potato as her speciality. It's been years since i've occupied the same physical space as my Father, and i don't know how my body will react. Pie might not be the best idea.

But i do have a few questions on my mind: Why do people keep saying i'm like him? That i look like him? Why would anyone say that? Also, i've seen my German birth certificate; i needed it when i joined the U.S. military. A mother's name is mentioned, but there's no father. What's that about?

My Father and i stand outside his apartment, on the balcony in the desert heat, so we can talk privately. He's wearing what i'll eventually call his around-the-house uniform, a white tank-top undershirt with suspenders holding up his shorts. All i feel is impatient.

My eyes are set on him. My arms are locked across my chest. My fingers squeeze my sides for comfort. He looks down, while keeping a respectable distance with his hands in his pockets. This is our inaugural adult conversation about anything of importance, and i'm waiting for answers.

He starts with a story.

"After Vietnam," he begins in his gravelly voice. It's the first time i notice he sounds like Papa Bear, and i can't say that i've really paid attention to its timbre before now. Over the phone, his voice hadn't sunk in. But in person, its vibration rumbles through me.

"After Vietnam, the doctors said i couldn't have kids. It was that Agent Orange. I didn't have no kinda problems like that before the war. After the war, I couldn't have kids."

Agent Orange is an herbicide used in large-scale U.S. military operations during the Vietnam War to destroy forest cover and crops. Intended to choke the enemy and starve the land, Agent Orange also rained down on American soldiers, and it didn't discriminate. It seeped into the soil, the water, and the bodies of everyone it touched.

American soldiers brought home the effects of Agent Orange in the form of multiple diseases recognized by the U.S. Department of Veterans Affairs. The "Agent Orange" section of the VA's Public Health website lists 19 conditions associated with exposure, from a variety of cancers to diabetes and hypertension.

Male infertility is not on the VA's official list of conditions, and research on the matter is mixed, but this isn't an academic review. Suffice to say my Father's story begins in his mid-20s with the belief, if not proof, that he can't have children. He's also married to a woman who can't have children. It's a loveless marriage that can't produce hope or joy.

Her reflex is shame. His reflex is infidelity.

"In the Army in Germany, we'd go out in the country for field training. Our unit would be in the field for weeks, training on weapons and so forth, and we stayed in the villages."

This, according to my Father, is how he came to meet and have an affair with my "real" mother, the 19-year-old White German woman who gave birth to me.

A Black man in the version of the South that bred my Father risked dismemberment and death for improper interactions with a White woman. American magazines in 1955 put this version of the South on blast, publishing open-casket photos of the mutilated body of 14-year-old Emmett Till, who was tortured, beaten and shot by White men in Mississippi for supposedly whistling at a White woman. An all-White jury acquitted the men of murder. A year later, they sold their admission of guilt to a magazine for profit.

My Father was 13 years old then. Just 13 years later, he's not in America anymore.

"How did you meet her? Do you remember her name?" i fact-check.

"It was a long time ago. I don't remember her full name," he answers with exasperation. As much as he drank, i say to myself, it's a wonder he remembers his own name.

"Anyway, she went by a nickname. That's what everybody called her." The nickname he recounts is the middle name of the woman noted on my birth certificate.

"It wasn't hard to meet a German girl. They wasn't afraid of Black men, like at home," he explains. "Any time my unit went on field training, I saw her. Then, one time I go out there, and she tells me she's pregnant. She wants me to leave my wife and marry her."

This is happening in 1968. Several possibilities don't yet exist. She can't terminate the pregnancy without risking her life. She can't keep a child without her family's support. And he can't test for paternity without involving the military and risking his career.

"I tell her ain't no way this baby is mine. I cain't even have kids," he says. "But she tells me it is, and if i don't marry her, she's gonna put you up for adoption."

"Wait, wait, wait," because i need a minute to process what i feel in my body as the worst possible thing he could be telling me. "YOU adopted me because I'm YOURS?"

"I wasn't gonna do anything, just let her give you up," he admits. "But guys in my unit, the Black guys, they told me Germany was just as racist as America. Even worse with the Nazis. You know they'd been runnin' things in Germany just 20 years before."

Yep, World War II, i'd heard of it.

"America got problems, but it's my country. I fought for this county. I couldn't leave my child in a racist foreign country. So I went to the lawyer handling the adoption, told him you were mine, and I wanted to adopt you."

He stops talking.

Repeatedly, i'd surrendered on my knees and asked that this man be forgiven for his sins against me. To do that, i did as my 12-stepper guide advised: i framed my Father as a stranger. Some random man who wound up with a child probably because his wife wanted one. A child for whom he had no foundational responsibility. A child to whom he owed nothing. Forgiveness had been predicated on him being a stranger.

But he's not a stranger. He's my got-damn father. His story blows my story apart.

What kind of a human being violates their own child?! It's another rhetorical question in the heat of an emotional moment. Clarity will come much later.

One more real question for now: "How the hell did you manage this with your wife?"

"I told her, I had a child. I was adopting you, and if she didn't wanna adopt this child with me, she could leave."

In the battles i'd seen between my Mother and Father, more often than not, my Mother struck the deciding blow. The idea that my Father put his foot down and put to his wife the impossible choice of either returning to Alabama unmarried or raising his bastard mixed-race child is unbelievable. Except i'm standing in front of him as the living result.

From here, my memory goes completely blank, i can't even guess at what i might've said. What i do recall is a reaction in my body so intense, within 2 days, i'm sitting in the waiting room of the local hospital with a wicked case of bronchitis. My chest is all twisted and tight, my lungs ache from coughing, and i can hardly breathe.

Sitting with me is my new father. Damn, i gotta do a whole new round of forgiveness.

His new wife has so much love to offer, she's leading a prayer circle with people we don't even know. At least this time around, forgiveness will keep me close to her love.

/ - .-. ..- - .... /

In July 2003, my Stepdad called to tell me it was time. My Mother had raged, smoked and drank her way into cancer that blew past chemotherapy and radiation, and spread through her body like wildfire.

As an abused child and infuriated teenager, this is exactly what i'd wished for her.

Fortunately, by the time this came to pass, i was an adult who practiced forgiveness.

The emotional weight of wishing a parent dead and having that parent literally die exactly as i'd wished could've sat on me for the rest of my life. Maybe i would've felt vindicated. Most likely, i would've felt guilty. Vindication or guilt, i can't say that either sustains a healthy heart, learner's mind, or loving spirit. Thankfully, i didn't feel either.

More often than not, when i choose to forgive, pieces of complicated life puzzles reveal themselves, and those revelations reinforce and validate the heavy work of forgiveness.

The Balcony Revelation about my complicated adoption happens because i'd forgiven my Father enough to stand in his presence and hear his truth.

That revelation also occurred within a year of moving on from my Mother. The timing gave me nearly 5 years to ruminate on her reality and reckon with her truth: a woman raised in violence; raped; robbed of her ability to conceive her own child; pragmatically resigned to a man she didn't love; physically battered; and saddled with adopting and raising the progeny of her drunken husband's infidelity.

Now i understood why she hated my Father. Now i knew why she didn't love me.

Those last 5 years, my Mother had the love of her life. She had an opportunity to heal, grow, and evolve. Her miracle was so close. But having also stood at the threshold of recovery, i know how terrifying change feels, like standing barefoot with the challenge of walking across a bed of hot coals. Incidentally, i did a barefoot coal-walk in my 20s, and i can still smell the smokey veil of terror i stepped through to get to the other side.

Vastly outnumbered by her trauma monsters, maybe my Mother's opportunities to be better were too little. Maybe they came too late.

Or maybe these are reasons, but there's no excuse. People overcome horrors and go on to create productive lives for themselves and loving environments for their families.

She could've done better. She should've done better.

The thing is, it ultimately doesn't matter what she could've or should've done because i can't (re)live her life, i can only live my life. My life isn't about her. My life is about me.

Do i spend the rest of my life blaming or condemning her? Who carries that blame and condemnation in their body? Who suffers from it?

For whatever could've or should've happened, all we got was a toxic trauma-bond. Love would've been a blessing, but it's not how life went down. My blessings were distance, time, and truth. They dissolved the bond. Forgiveness kept me clear of it.

So when my Stepdad reached out, i had the emotional capacity to move into their home and see after her for the final 6 weeks of her life.

My Mother was my first experience with a parent dying at home. She's how i learned about in-home care, hospice, morphine, and hospital beds. It was on-the-job training that i would put to good use again, and again, for the Parents i love.

Her transition also provided my first experience of what reconciliation looks like.

By reconciliation, i don't mean letting things go and getting back together. Genuine reconciliation, as i know it, is an experience of peace with the past. Wrongs and truth are honored and leveraged for learning. Differences that painfully divided find their rest.

We can't rightly do reconciliation if wrongs aren't in the past, or we're not ready for peace. When she was living, my Mother couldn't move beyond the past, and she couldn't exist in peace. Her continued toxicity meant i couldn't have her in my life.

Reconciliation was not on the table then. Change had to wait until she was truly dying.

When i first arrived, my Mother asked me for a cigarette and a beer. A smoker since the age of 13, she already had cancer everywhere, she reasoned. No point in quitting now.

Week over week, she lost her body. She couldn't walk, go to the bathroom, or eat solid foods. In her physical deterioration, my Mother's addictions and afflictions also abated.

She no longer craved nicotine, alcohol, and rage. Likely for the first time since her own childhood, she wasn't anxious, suffering, or terrified.

The closer she got to death, the more she regressed to a carefree essence.

She was safe, protected, and playful - all the things our inner child should be.

When i tripped and threw a protein shake all over her, and the hospital bed, and the ceiling, she made up a rhyme and sang about it:

OOP-sy daisy, on the CEI-ling

OOP-sy daisy, what a FEE-ling

It's the first sweet-spirited song she'd ever sung to me as my Mother.

Her 6 weeks of transition were demanding with 24-hour care, but there was goodness in them. The house was calm, she was well-tended to, and i could quietly reread books she'd kept from my childhood. These turned out to be the best days of our relationship.

My Stepdad, who died 3 years later in 2006, was hospitalized with heart problems and missed his wife's last 2 weeks. It seemed fated, having it come down to her and me.

If she'd had it her way, my Mother would've died in a motel in her 30s and left me on my own at 13. As the woman who raised me, her role in my life was to keep me alive long enough to release me to the world. It would've been too soon for the both of us.

Instead, she got to die in the comfort of her home, with me present to see it through.

My Mother didn't like or love me. The feeling was mostly mutual. We weren't mother and daughter so much as we were each other's minder: her at the start of my life, me at the end of hers.

Still, empathy came. So did appreciation, reconciliation, and closure. All of it followed forgiveness – for who she was; for who she wasn't; and most of all, for me.

Roots, Truths & Turning Points

- *How do you tend to refer to the people who've raised or shaped you? What's behind those naming choices?*

- *What's a belief, fact, or story from your upbringing that you either needed to hold on to or let go of to become who you are now?*

- *In what ways have you experienced forgiveness without reconciliation? Or reconciliation without forgiveness? What does the distinction mean for you?*

10. FORGIVENESS FALLACIES

When forgiveness showed up in my early adulthood, it met a brick wall of resistance constructed from fallacy: i'd never made any effort to forgive anyone, but i had a host of dysfunctionally formed thoughts and feelings about what might happen if i did.

A fallacy is a mistaken belief or flawed conclusion arising unintentionally from a lack of understanding or faulty reasoning. In other words, fallacies result when we don't know enough to know better. We can be right to some degree but still holding onto a fallacy.

My categorical dismissal of forgiveness as a weakness wasn't wrong, but it was most definitely a flawed conclusion based on dysfunctional experience and damaged logic.

The context and conditions of forgiveness are a highly consequential bit of detail that i didn't know to consider. Forgiveness in compromising conditions can put us in harm's way. If my forgiveness process had required interacting with my Father, or if my Father had asked my forgiveness but demonstrated no intention to rectify his behavior - these conditions no doubt would have created vulnerability and violation.

Fortunately for me, the 12-stepper who shaped my forgiveness process was directive and protective. My Father was nowhere near my forgiveness experience, and i didn't need to engage with him to practice forgiveness and discover release.

A powerful alchemizer, forgiveness proved strong enough on its own to transform my resentment into acceptance, my hate into love, and (eventually) my Father into my Dad.

"Forgiveness is a weakness" is so far from truth, i'm grateful i cleared this mindset early in adulthood. Along my way, i've tackled a few other questionable forgiveness fallacies.

/ ..-. .- .-.. .-.. .- -.-. -.-- /

To err is human, to forgive is divine

Making mistakes is part of being human. Choosing to forgive lifts us closer to grace.

Totally get that. Framing forgiveness as divine also implies a saintly activity for the spiritually advanced, and this implication can be problematic.

The sanctimonious "i'm just gon' pray for you and not process how pissed off i am" emotionally suppressive behavior that can come along with divine forgiveness pushes it into fallacy territory for me.

For those of us wrestling with betrayal or trauma, there's implicit expectation in divine forgiveness to rise above human emotions. It negates the reality of being human – like saying it's OK to cry, but it's gross to blow your nose afterward. Humans gotta human.

These rise-above expectations can also silence pain and set us up for continued harm.

Positioning forgiveness as the ultimate virtue might, for example, compel someone to offer it before they're ready, or without genuine resolution, simply to meet a lofty ideal.

The way we forgive doesn't need to be conciliatory, peacemaking, or polite.

Recalling the high-road church folks of my childhood, promoting forgiveness as divine risks turning forgiveness into a shiny, moral badge instead of a practical healing tool.

Forgiveness may be divine, but i can't reach my healing if it's high up on a pedestal.

For me, forgiveness isn't a moral or religious issue, it's an emotional and mental health issue. Forgiveness isn't a holy thing we *have* to do to be a good people. It's a life tool we use on our own terms to become healthier people.

/ ..-. .- .-.. .-.. .- -.-. -.-- /

People need to ask and/or earn forgiveness before we forgive

This idea has some truth in it, but it also misdirects us outward, rather than inward.

As long as our forgiveness rests on actions, apologies, or admissions of wrongdoing from others, our power to heal, grow and move forward sits with them, not within us.

My forgiveness experiences tell me we don't need to engage someone who hurt us to forgive. Forgiveness worked for me precisely because it didn't need to involve anyone.

We don't need to extend our forgiveness to others in order to practice forgiveness. We need only be open to forgiveness as a practice that supports how we're trying to live.

If forgiveness doesn't need to be extended outward to positively impact our own lives, then we need not concern ourselves with someone else's asks or earns.

We need only resist a bit less, put forgiveness to the test, and release in our own time.

/ ..-. .- .-.. .-.. .- -.-. -.-- /

Forgive and forget

Forgetting is not a flex. If we suffer harm, turning our back on our memories doesn't leave us better off emotionally. Quite the opposite, it can mean ignoring or bypassing our pain, abandoning ourselves emotionally, and setting ourselves up for violation.

Wonder why we're triggered? Because we don't forget.

Maybe we think we've forgotten, but our nervous systems log and catalog every harm and every foul. In 12-step, i once heard someone crippled by depression share how the majority of their childhood memories had been obliterated by their alcohol use: "I know something's wrong with me, but I don't know what it is. I wish I could remember."

Their debilitating mental health issues lived on, long after their memories were gone.

Still, because the grass is always greener, i found myself listening to this 12-stepper and thinking but not saying: "Man, I remember EVERYTHING. I wish I could forget."

In the chaos of my early adulthood, i did my messy best to blank out the past, but it persisted and stayed ever-present in my body. So visceral and permanent is its imprint, there are still sounds and smells – screaming children, cigarette smoke – i can't stand from childhood. Ultimately, i had to forgive because my body could not forget.

Maybe you're of the mind that if we forgive and don't forget, we're holding a grudge. But if you refuse to remember, then how do you learn? Remembering is how we retain life-preserving insight about what nurtures, sustains and supports us. And what does not. It's how we care for ourselves. Forgiveness isn't a magic reset button. If and when forgiveness happens, it's most effectively accompanied by boundaries, not amnesia.

Forgive and forget can work in the short-term, but it only gets us so far in the journey from hurt to healed.

The problem with forgiveness isn't forgiveness. It's our flawed framing of forgiveness, our fallacies, handicapping our ability to heal and grow through what's wounded us.

Inability and unwillingness to forgive may serve us, but that doesn't mean they help us.

For sustainable adulting, maybe we forget the fallacies, maybe upgrade and replace them with more effective alternatives.

Surrender and forgive. Forgive and release. Forgive and transform. Forgive and be free.

Fallacies Aside

- *Which of your forgiveness fallacies showed up in this chapter? Or what's one fallacy you've had that wasn't repped here?*

- *Reframing forgiveness, how would you explain your version of it to someone who's just getting their grown-up life started, or someone who's new to it?*

- *How do you know when you're ready to forgive? Or is readiness even part of forgiveness for you?*

11. DIVORCE MOUNTAIN

There's a friend who came into my life right around the time that he and i were walking through divorces neither of us had expected or wanted. The dissolution of my marriage began in Spring 2021, a season before his. Our circumstances differed, but we were navigating the same life-loss and feeling our way through mutually recognizable pain.

In my case, the marriage had ended just as the 10-year relationship reached its zenith.

Year 7 had been the rockiest. Though we happily belonged to each other, throughout 2018, we were persistently at odds. There was a pile-up of harms over matters large and small, and we had no guide or guidance for navigating and clearing the way.

In our dynamic, i was a tough unstoppable force pushing her beyond her comfort zone. She was a headstrong immovable object, unable to trust anyone's thinking as much as her own. She would do a thing that i experienced as an instigation. My fierce reaction would then fuel an escalation. Our sharp tones, careless words and divergent needs would cut us off from each other.

The 7-Year Itch, that idiomatic timeframe when long-term couples start rubbing each other the wrong way, had shown up for us with masterful clockwork precision.

It didn't help that we were Californians with tech jobs, doing the Silicon Valley grind of commute and work and work and work. Professional life gobbled up our weekdays and left us spent on weekends. She came up with *Friday Night Introvert Dance Party* as a cheeky brand for our habit of heading to bed around the time other adults headed out.

Along with having little time or energy for each other, we each had our own individual issues surface in Year 7 that existentially threatened our couplehood.

On her side, she'd awakened to the realization that she wanted to live independently. In our early years, she shared how she'd imagined being married for life like her parents, who met in high school. Now, she didn't want to be responsibly attached to someone. She'd gone from her parents' home to being in college to being in a relationship with me. Now, she wanted to be with herself.

On my side, that summer, a talk therapist diagnosed me with complex PTSD.

/ -.. .. ...- --- .-. -.-. . /

In my previous 20+ years of self-development, no therapist who'd heard the harrowing particulars of my childhood had ever identified my experience as trauma or recognized post-traumatic stress disorder as a condition undermining my functionality as an adult.

It'd taken a new millennium for a mental health care professional to finally figure it out.

The Maryland-based National Center for Trauma-Informed Care didn't exist until 2005. In the decades since, across various fields of health care, a host of trauma types have been named, normalized, and socialized, including (but not limited to):

- acute trauma: typically associated with a single event that happens in one's life e.g. car accident, theft, a physical or sexual assault, a school shooting, and other experiences that threaten an individual's physical and/or emotional safety
- collective or mass trauma: large-scale natural and human-caused disasters and events involving significant loss

of property and lives, and widespread disruption of normal routines and services e.g. 9/11, Hurricane Katrina, COVID-19

- developmental trauma: adverse events and experiences of childhood
- historical trauma: multi-generational harm experienced by a specific cultural, racial or ethnic group e.g. the Vietnam War, American slavery, the Holocaust
- intergenerational trauma: events and experiences within a single family across generations e.g. poverty, imprisonment, forced migration
- life-transition trauma: these events are a natural part of living but nonetheless can undermine one's sense of certainty, safety and self e.g. illness or medical conditions, a relative's passing, a pet's death, job loss, a divorce
- relational trauma: physical or psychological harm in relationships that don't reliably offer safety, stability, love, respect, validation, support, or caregiving e.g. domestic violence, emotional abuse, addiction issues, elder neglect or abuse
- vicarious trauma: indirect exposure to traumatic events e.g. first-responders, journalists, family and friends who witness or hear stories of others' trauma

So varied and prevalent are the types of trauma we encounter, some mental health thought-leaders and practitioners (Bessel van der Kolk, Gabor Maté, Judith Herman, Peter Levine, Resmaa Menakem) insist trauma is not an exceptional experience but rather a foundational aspect of being human.

You may think you've never had a trauma experience, but according to some who've devoted their life's work to thinking about this, being human is the trauma experience.

These days, "trauma" is prevalent enough in common vernacular to be casually used as a synonym for everyday mishaps such as losing one's keys or a barista flubbing a coffee order. A standout moment during my stint in tech was overhearing a colleague seriously lament the trauma of the company cafeteria running out of breakfast burritos.

Those of us who truly know trauma can hear ourselves attuned to its debilitating truth: The world is fundamentally unsafe, and we are fundamentally unsafe in the world.

Not everyone who experiences a trauma event continues to view the world as unsafe long after the trauma event has passed. But more than a few of us do. When that's so, it's a likely indication of post-traumatic stress disorder.

PTSD presents as an unrelenting plague of life-impairing symptoms. Nightmares and sleeplessness, intrusive memories, flashbacks, excessive avoidance of situations and people, and distempered reactivity e.g. hypervigilance, excessive irritability, rage - this is a short list of the hell on offer.

Mental health practitioners further distinguish between PTSD and complex PTSD by how much and how many types of trauma a person has experienced. The more varied and long-lasting the trauma, the more likely PTSD's severity will intensify into c-PTSD.

It's the difference between being haunted by 1 or 2 trauma monsters versus an entire village of trauma monsters. There's just that much more work to do to exorcise them.

Folks with PTSD are easy to dismiss and hard to meet with empathy. Brusquely put, we're the assholes of the world. We're ill-tempered, rude, difficult, angry, and scary.

Like animals caught in a trap, we're also fragile, vulnerable, injured, and in pain.

Next time you encounter someone who loses their shite over a relatively small thing, ask yourself: "Is this potentially PTSD?" Because when you live with PTSD, you're on constant red alert. And when you're on constant red alert, there are NO small things.

/ -.. .. ...- --- .-. -.-. . /

My spouse was a person of nurturing and calm; i was a person of power and strength. We were yin and yang when our complementarity worked, oil and water when it didn't.

My c-PTSD had been a hard thing for her soft spirit to handle. By Year 7, neither of us could say for certain whether her desire for independence stemmed from a need to not be married at all, or a need to not be married to me.

When i got my c-PTSD diagnosis, i didn't know what i needed, but i knew it wouldn't be enough to sit on a talk therapist's couch and process. All the self-work i'd done to excavate addiction, dysfunction and depression, and STILL, i had trauma monsters fused to my bones – i needed to get free of them before i lost everything that mattered.

Shortly after my c-PTSD diagnosis, my spouse and i visited a California hot springs i'd been retreating to since my late-20s. As we checked in, i noticed this new book on the front desk, *Psychedelic Medicine: The Healing Powers of LSD, MDMA, Psilocybin, and Ayahuasca.* Published in 2017, the book was a collection of interviews with researchers exploring the therapeutic potential of psychedelics for mental health. Dr. Richard Louis Miller, its author, also happened to be the founder of my favorite respite from humanity.

In the course of a weekend, i went from having never done psychedelics and knowing nothing about them to insisting i had to start doing psychedelics as soon as possible.

Year 7 ended with me taking up psychedelic-assisted therapy in no small part thanks to a serendipitous conversation that my normally private and risk-averse spouse had with a coworker. He was a software engineer who, during a lunchtime walk, shared steps he was taking to leave tech and become a therapist who could work with psychedelics.

She told him about my c-PTSD and how i'd been seeking access to psychedelic-based treatment. Not an easy thing to find, given the substances were illegal and unregulated.

Setting aside her typical reserve, she asked if he knew someone who could help me. Trusting her honesty, he connected me to a therapist from an underground community of practitioners who leveraged psychedelic substances as mental health medicines.

A trained psychologist, my therapist supported me with a combination of talk therapy and daylong psychedelic journeys, guided experiences with mind-altering substances.

Central to the 20-ish (i legit lost count) psychedelic journeys i undertook in 5 years was my therapist's commitment to set, setting, intention, and integration. Referred to as the container, this structured approach and protective frame optimized for my physical and psychological safety, and reduced risk. It also accelerated my ability to rewire my brain, mend my heart, and transfer my breakthroughs from the psychedelic realm into real life.

For the uninitiated, here's how i experienced the container's components:

Set is short for mindset e.g. emotional readiness, fear, expectations. Our internal state can amplify insight or distress in a journey. Self-awareness is key for a fruitful voyage.

Setting is the external environment e.g. location, people, sounds, energy. Where we are and who we're with significantly impact our safety and influence a journey's vibe.

Intention is a guiding purpose or inquiry that orients the journey and leads to insights. This clear *why* is an anchor we can hold onto to steady ourselves through the journey.

Integration is where the work and wonders happen. If we question, explore and apply journeywork to our everyday lives, we can turn a trippy experience into lifelong change.

Psychedelic-assisted therapy did for me in 5 years what several years of talk therapy alone hadn't. It shifted entirely how my childhood lived in me. It also uprooted my rage, replacing it with an internal operating system running on connection and compassion.

Not that i got all carefree and kumbaya about the human experience, but i did stop resenting us as a species, and i stopped getting spun up in the drama of our times.

Set, setting, intention and integration turbo-transformed c-PTSD into post-traumatic healing and growth. Once i no longer qualified for a PTSD diagnosis, i closed out my psychedelic-assisted therapy, but i held on to this structured approach for progress.

Now, even without psychedelics, when i come up against a challenge or change, i pull out the container and put whatever's happening inside. Worldwide pandemic, fear, and uncertainty? Inside the container. The death of my Parents? Inside the container.

When i'm focused on the (mind)set, setting, intention and integration i need to support myself through an experience, i can keep calm and carry on, stay present and level up.

The container transcended my journeys to become an indispensable tool for healing, growth, and personal evolution. Being human, sometimes, it's just so hard. When i put life travails inside the container, i can safely and effectively make hard and heavy times make sense, make them mean something productive, and make them transformative.

If not for the container, i might've collapsed under the weight of one of the heaviest times of my adult life, the gut-punching loss of a marriage i thought had been saved.

/ -.. .. ...- --- .-. -.-. . /

As i was getting into psychedelic-assisted therapy at the end of Year 7, i also learned from Alain de Botton that my spouse and i had each married the wrong person.

Botton is a philosopher and co-founder of The School of Life, an organization focused on emotional intelligence and practical philosophy for everyday life. Shared in 2014 on The School's YouTube channel, Botton's marriage views went mainstream in America when

The New York Times published his thoughts as an opinion piece in 2016. In 2017, Botton had a hot minute in tech when Google hosted him in Silicon Valley for a talk.

In short, Botton told us that we'd married the wrong person for two reasons: because we didn't know ourselves well enough to know what we truly needed; and because we seek familiarity, to include the familiar suffering and pain bred into us from childhood.

Estimates of U.S. divorce rates have varied the past 10 years from 30-ish% to 50% or more, depending on your internet source. Whatever the actual double-digit percentage, the fact that the rate is indeed a double-digit told me that Botton was on to something.

Divorce was a nuclear option neither my spouse nor i were up for right away. Anyways, we didn't need a divorce to be rid of our problematic marriage. We needed a change to how we were doing marriage. If the one we'd made wasn't working, i suggested to my home renovations-loving spouse, let's scrap it and figure out how to build a better one.

Years 8 and 9 we spent in couples therapy, airing our grievances, understanding our dynamics, and developing new ways to listen and talk to each other. While parking at our therapist's office, we'd often ask: "Whose turn do you think it is to cry this week?"

We learned to see our disagreements through the roles on the drama triangle, a model describing our human predilection for purposely abdicating personal power (Victims), finding and assigning fault and blame (Villains), or rescuing and fixing others (Heroes).

Image by Jason R. Waller

Don't get it twisted. The use of victim-villain-hero descriptors in the context of the drama triangle is narrow, specific, and not to be overinterpreted. No one is saying or suggesting here that victims, villains and heroes aren't real.

Our personal power can be stolen and overridden, rendering us victims. Predators and abusers unequivocally qualify as villains. People who lay down their lives for the sake of others are undeniable heroes. That's reality.

The drama triangle is talking about roles we play based on mindsets we assume and assign, as well as patterns we're drawn into for attention, control, or validation.

Are we actually helpless and powerless with nothing we can do to better a situation for ourselves? Or are we giving our power away through learned helplessness?

Are blame and fault really the heart of the matter? Or is personal responsibility a more relevant - and a more adult - consideration?

Do we come to the rescue solely in service of others who can't help themselves? Or is our showing up as the Good Guy kind of more about ourselves?

The drama triangle is basically that toxic group chat energy where nobody in the room seems able to own how their behavior creates or exacerbates a challenging situation.

It's also kind of like The Matrix. Once you see it, you can't unsee it.

At home, at work, in families, in politics, in relationships of all kinds, the stories we're telling each other and ourselves about what's happening and why are rife with victims and villains and heroes – all stirring up drama and making matters worse.

Before awareness, i tended to vacillate between villain and hero, escalating a conflict, then setting about solving it for everyone, whether you wanted me to or not. The hero move was my codependency in action, trying to fix you so you didn't leave or hurt me.

Particularly with my spouse, though, there was another layer of wounded tendency that the drama triangle didn't quite capture.

What i experienced as her instigations were moments of behavior that tripped a primal fear in me of being unloved or unsafe. In those moments when my fears were inflamed and acute, i'd jump off the drama triangle and onto what i dubbed my trauma triangle.

In my journal, i drew it like so:

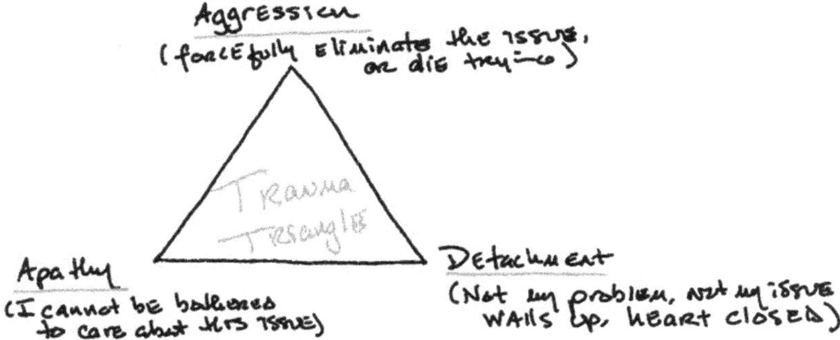

If planting my flag and dying on a hill of unrelenting argument didn't change a situation, then i'd either coldly refuse to care about people and their problems in the first place, or i'd detach and disengage, like Homer Simpson fading into the bushes.

In therapy, i learned to recognize my trauma triangle escalations as trauma responses. The point of them was to push away from my spouse as a pain source and protect me from this person with whom i felt most vulnerable.

Getting a handle on my own trauma-healing subsequently energized and expanded my capacity for repairing and renovating my marriage. It took concerted effort and a bunch of missteps, but the work eventually bore fruit. Stories in my head about my spouse's behavior started to change. My behavior started to mature. My last recorded trauma response occurred in May 2020, a full year before my spouse asked me for a divorce.

After 2 years of collective work, our therapist pronounced us "high-functioning" and confidently sent us on our way. We'd done it! We'd successfully rebuilt our marriage into a healthy partnership. We communicated effectively. We collaborated successfully. We loved each other affectionately. We'd changed our stars, and we were doing great.

But my spouse wasn't.

We had our therapist, and i had my therapist, but she didn't have anyone, and i let that be OK. We'd agreed to always, so i was counting on plenty of time for us to develop at our own pace. My lesson learned: couple's work in no way replaces individual work.

Though i knew my former spouse in ways she didn't know herself, there were shades of her i didn't know at all, not even after 10 years. Those shades ended our marriage.

People who knew us as a couple were taken aback - and vicariously traumatized - by the news, which i shared sparingly. In the first 6 months, the only people i told were a handful of folks who were close to me, plus a few folks who'd been close to us as a couple. One friend burst into tears when i told them, reminded as they were of a buddy who spent a year leaning toward suicide after his wife unexpectedly quit their marriage.

The rest of my phone call with that friend i spent reassuring us both that i'd somehow get through this divorce, and we all would be OK.

Well into my 40s by the time i got married, i'd done enough self-work to avoid obvious dysfunctional pitfalls from my upbringing – the violence, addiction, chaos and whatnot.

So it wasn't immediately apparent to me what i hadn't known about what i needed as a person, or what childhood pain my relationship had been replicating.

What i did know to do was put the divorce in the container of set, setting, intention and integration. To start, i set my mind on the notion that there would be no victims, villains, or heroes in my divorce. There was grief, anger, despair. But there would be no drama.

People were infuriated on my behalf, and just about everyone took sides. For those on Team Me, she was the villain. Even a friend of mine who operates from a vast reserve of care and compassion drifted onto the drama triangle by inquiring so politely when i broke the news: "Is it too early to say something unkind about her?"

With my mind set, i persistently insisted that, though vows had been violated and injury had been sustained, she was not the villain, nor was i the victim. Each of us had our proverbial 50 cents in the dollar of our demise. Which is to say that both of us were challenged human beings doing the best we could do.

Neither of us had been victimized. Neither of us needed to be vilified.

Hurt as i was about the demise of my marriage, it was also clear from the outset that forgiving her - for being unable to heal with me or be happy with us - would make it that much easier to forgive myself for being unable to achieve the one outcome i most wanted for myself: a safe and healthy family.

If she could be forgiven her shortcomings in our relationship, then so could i.

/ -.. .. ...- --- .-. -.-. . /

Divorce knocked me to my knees, but i still had the power to pull myself to my feet.

Putting the divorce in the container, i held an intention to minimize interactions with my soon-to-be former spouse and bring my best self to our necessary exchanges. Once the divorce was in motion, there was no point processing further about the relationship. Engaging would only worsen the injury, and my feelings were no longer her business.

We worked out terms over email, and though she made twice as much money as i did, i asked nothing of her beyond swift and peaceful resolution. She initiated the divorce, so she offered to pay for an attorney. We'd been traveling separately the week we had her "I want a divorce" conversation. First to return, me and my best self neatly packed the bulk of her belongings, then left town the week she moved out of our shared space.

Also, i refused to make her my Ex. Consider the sound. For me, it mimics the letter X marking a trouble spot. Allowing her to occupy and live rent-free on troubled terrain in my internal landscape? Hard pass.

She was my soon-to-be former spouse, that was a fact. But she would not be my Ex. That felt like a choice.

For setting, i assembled what i called my Life Team to wrap around and keep me safe, mostly from myself. This included welcoming support from someone i'd known since college who had traversed this same rocky terrain a year before me, someone i came to depend on like a divorce sherpa to get me safely up Divorce Mountain.

When i could feel the pain and anger about to drive me out of my mind – like 8 weeks in, when my soon-to-be former spouse bought a house to start her life without me, and i thought, yeah, i should go set it on fire and burn it down – i could call my sherpa first.

In this instance, my sherpa trekked me back around to my best-self intention, but also offered to roll with me if i still thought the house-burning idea was a good one after a night's sleep. For the record, i did not.

Back in my home alone, repair needs serendipitously connected me to my new friend, hired initially as a pair of handy hands. We met when i was incapable of surface-level small talk for more than 5 minutes. As he staple-gunned outdoor carpet to my balcony, we learned about the dissolution of each other's marriages and dove into the deep end of each other's lives. It was immediately clear we were gonna see each other through the hardest parts of our ordeals and be around on the other side to talk about them.

In his case, and in contrast to mine, his marriage ended at its nadir. A third person had been involved, and a marriage that started with vows of fidelity and forever devolved into betrayal and a couple tearing at each other in a bitter battle over how it would end.

His split was as acrimonious as mine was amicable. Like me and my former spouse, they didn't have children, pets or plants together. Unlike me and my former spouse, they fought over money, material possessions, and who owed what to whom.

In the grip of recovering from a heart attack, my friend nonetheless refused to relent.

He wanted retribution and recompense. He had an Ex, and he needed his Ex to suffer. Years later, he'd taken up the sweet company of a kind-hearted woman and moved on with his life, but this need still simmered in him.

We talked about forgiveness as i wrote this book, 4 years after our divorces had been finalized. He didn't even have to say his Ex's name for me to know she'd come to mind.

He hunched and curled his shoulders, folding his hulking frame in on itself. His arms crossed his chest, blocking his heart. His brow furrowed under his baseball cap. His head slowly shook from side to side with deliberate nonverbal resistance.

"She doesn't effin' deserve it, man," he insisted. "You can't forgive somebody when they don't deserve it." His pain argued on his behalf, aiming to protect him, instead holding him back.

"Dude, you deserve it. You deserve to forgive her and be free of . . . all this," i said, hand-gesturing at the obvious hurt in his body. "I mean, what's the alternative? You gonna romance your resentment for the rest of your life?"

"I love my resentment," he chuckled while giving himself a bear hug.

"Alright, Dude, date your hate if you want. But it hurts you, not her," i cautioned as i pointed to his literally over-taxed heart.

"Oh I forgive myself for getting into that disaster and not seeing what I shoulda seen, but she needs to suffer." He just couldn't relent. "I need her to suffer for what she did."

"The thing about that," i offered, "is that as long as you hold this need for her to suffer, you're still holding her."

He nodded his head a bit but didn't say anything further, and since i'm his friend, not his therapist, i let the conversation rest.

One of us will go on romancing our resentment and dating our hate. The other of us will keep deciding in favor of forgiveness.

Gear Check for the Climb

- *What challenge in your life could you put inside the container of set, setting, intention, and integration i.e. what could benefit from a shift in your thinking, surroundings, support, focus, purpose, and learning?*

- *Who's got your back when things get hard? Do you have a life team you can count on? Or is it time to build one?*

- *Get honest – are you romancing a resentment or dating a hate? When emotions flare or tensions rise, where do you land on the drama triangle? Do you blame, fix, escalate? What might help you to step off the triangle and own your part? What might open up if you finally let all of it go?*

12. YOU DECIDE

Noodling on forgiveness with a friend over lunch, i was asked my thoughts about their situation: "Do you need to forgive to move forward? Like, the problem has fully passed, and you're not in the same context with the person? Do you think you need to forgive?"

Replacing "I" with a "you" is a classic verbal tic in American English. It lets us deflect and maintain emotional distance when we're talking about our hard things. When i hear people use "you" instead of "I" in conversation, i tend to turn the focus around. My aim is to get people to (re)connect with themselves, their truth, and their own inner wisdom.

So i asked: "What do *you* think you need to do? Do you think these questions would be alive in you if there wasn't something there for you about forgiveness?"

What i think is you don't need me telling you whether you need to forgive, and no one can definitively tell you if you *need* to forgive. If you're wondering about forgiveness, maybe there's something more to explore. Listen to your questions, and convictions.

As Botton points out in his marriage guidance, we often don't know what we need, but we do tend to go on about what we want. This starts early in us. Tune into the language of little kids. They typically don't ask for what they need. They demand what they want.

Coming out of a subway station one day long ago in Berlin, i found myself walking behind a German-speaking mother and her preschooler. The Little One was trying to walk and talk simultaneously, and it was proving more arduous than he could handle.

Unable to locate and articulate his words, his little brain got stuck repeatedly on the phrase: "*Ich will . . . Ich will . . . Ich will* – I want . . . I want . . . I want."

His mother, shoulders sagging at the end of the day, held his hand and shuffled along at his short-leg pace of a stair-step at a time. With an exhausted sigh, she countered, "*Ja ich weiss, du willst, du willst, du willst* – yes I know, you want, you want, you want."

This, i thought, is what humans must sound like to the Universe: I want. I want. I want. We're at times so mired in our persistent wants, we can be blind to our pressing needs. These blind spots are what i hear when people throw up anti-forgiveness alternatives:

I want them to suffer.

I want them to pay.

As you know by now, i get this – i've wanted a parent to suffer and pay for what they did to me. But i wanted this why? Because it validated my pain? Because it was plain wrong that someone could hurt me, then carry on having a good life? Because justice?

First off, if i'd been able to pay any attention or know anything about how the world works, i'd have known that my Mother was already suffering. She was violent, poor, and dependent on a man she didn't love. These are not the ingredients of a good life.

The White men who killed Emmet Till, and did no prison time for their crime, eventually lost the store where Till was accused of whistling at a White woman because Black folks stopped patronizing it. The men left Mississippi in infamy, and even though they returned, they didn't make it past the age of 63. They both suffered and died of cancer.

My proverbial Captain Justice cape hangs in a closet in my mind, ready for action. But as i've gotten older, and experienced repeatedly how seeking retribution rarely makes anything turn out well for me, i've learned to let the Universe sort out sins and sinners.

When we want someone to suffer, that's our prayer for them. They're probably already suffering, but if they aren't suffering obviously or enough to our liking, this is what we're using our life force on. We're spending energy from our food and sleep on positive declarations for someone else's demise. What does that cost us? What do we gain?

If we spent that energy on ourselves, what could we accomplish for our own lives?

In reality, we do love our resentments, as long as we feel them protecting us. By the time we notice they're actually eating us alive, we're often too attached to let them go.

If someone cares enough to call out where you might be romancing your resentment or dating your hate, it may make sense to pay attention to their observation. If there's legit concern you're doing a disservice to your life with a want for someone else's suffering, perhaps consider whether you and your resentment need a break from each other, you know, maybe see other people for a while.

Now, some of y'all who are much better humans than me, you don't want anyone to suffer. You just want what's fair, what's right:

I want them to realize how they hurt me.

I want them to be accountable.

I want them to make amends.

I want them to care.

That's what we want, really, for others to care about our pain and contribute to healing it with us or for us.

And. They. Can't.

Why?

In no small part because, not only are they also in pain, they don't even know how to solve for their own pain. In what world should someone who can't solve for their own pain be capable of solving for our pain?

For optimists who operate from how the world *should* work, this is especially difficult. Surely if you encountered someone in pain, you'd help them, right? People should help each other. People should care about each other's pain.

Except, reality. So, accept reality.

Other people, especially those who've hurt us, cannot care about our pain as we want. They can't give us what we need. Also, and more importantly, us expecting they should is a mirror reflecting our own challenge. If people should care about our pain in spite of theirs, should we not care about their pain in spite of ours? If we can't rise above and solve for their pain, why should they be any more capable of that than we are?

The help we want others to give us is the help calling out for us to give to ourselves.

My guidance, dissatisfying as it may sound, is that you do for yourself what you want others to do for you. Entertain the notion that a forgiveness practice could do for you the good that other people – godbless'em – simply don't have it in them to do.

/ -.. . -.-. .. -.. . /

If you are untroubled by resentment or resistance, it might truly be the case that you don't need a focus on forgiveness. It's not my purpose or (anyone's) place to convince you otherwise, only to encourage and assure you that, if you need to, you will be able to forgive anything. And, you will undoubtedly be better for it.

You get to decide if it's worthwhile for you to forgive. You are the one who grants yourself the permission you need to forgive. You are the one who decides whom you forgive. You might not start with someone else. You might start with forgiving yourself.

If you decide forgiveness might do you some good, what i can offer are my tools for navigating and transforming the pain of life into healing and growth that serve you.

The tools i use for this work are neither proprietary nor rocket science. They're a set of realistic and readily available ways to unhook from resentment, rewrite our pain stories, and return to wholeness and freedom, one moment at a time.

You may not believe you've ever been whole or free, or that it's possible to be whole or free. But you have, and it is. Your internal system remembers when you weren't buried and bound, and it's seeking relief and resolution.

Why else would you still be listening to me bang on in this book about forgiveness?

We don't often come to this work out of want. We're drawn to it out of need. If you're curious about forgiveness, it may be because forgiveness is on the lookout for you.

If it finds you, buckle up. This isn't a feel-good approach for awakening your vision and manifesting your dreams. This is forgiveness. This is internal peacemaking. This is work.

Forgiveness is an uncomfortable commitment to tackle resentments and resistance. Like deadlifting weights or marathon running, when you practice forgiveness, you're strengthening your ability to take on everyday life.

How can this be anything but uncomfortable? We're clearing hard shite.

No hard shite to clear? Then, yeah, go awaken and manifest. But if forgiveness is what you've decided you need, then get yourself geared up for work. Expect and accept that healing is hard, plan how you'll take good care of yourself, and fortheloveofgod, do not go it alone. Give yourself some support.

Also, these tools are *my* approach, not *the* approach, to forgiveness. They may not be the approach you stay with after you put some time into honing your forgiveness skills.

But if you don't have an effective approach for forgiveness, maybe give mine a try.

OK, with that said, here are the 4 tools i recommend to get you started on forgiveness.

Boundaries. When i refer to boundaries, i'm talking about vital self-protective limits that define the treatment i will not accept in order to preserve my safety and dignity.

Boundaries keep us from co-signing or colluding in activity that hurts us. For example, we don't require ourselves to forgive someone or something because it's the moral or right thing to do. Especially if you're being harmed physically, emotionally or spiritually, this is not the time for the moral high ground. This is the time for boundaries.

Back in my early recovery, my childhood Mother and Father each harangued me at some point about my refusal to be in an up-close relationship with them. My Mother insisted i had no business just thinking of myself, after all she'd done to raise me. My Father rang me while intoxicated to complain about me not being in touch.

"I don't call you because I don't want to have anything to do with you," i stated. "You molested me as a kid, you damaged me, and I don't want anything to do with you."

Drunk and in denial, my Father insisted, "I ain't never done nothing like that."

"You sayin' I'm lying?!" i fired back, then caught myself. "No. I know what happened. You do, too. Lucky for me, my life now doesn't need to have anything to do with you."

My childhood parents' behavior cemented the boundaries i set as a buffer between us to make room for my recovery. Holding my ground with them was a matter of survival.

From my perspective, it's safety before forgiveness.

People might insist you're being selfish or self-centered. Don't be gaslit or guilt-tripped into giving up your safety and well-being. Boundaries are you saying: "I'm not available for harm. I'm gonna do what's needed to protect my peace, safety, and sense of self."

A related question i've been asked is whether and how we can forgive someone if harm is continuing and ongoing. Before we go there, i'd first want to confirm whether we're talking about harm or hurt.

From experience and exploration, i understand hurt as the impact that can result from intentional and unintentional one-off or infrequent acts. Harm, however, implies deeper and lasting damage from actions that are both intentional and repeated.

A mom who loses her temper and whacks her child on the bottom, for example, likely hurts the Little One in more ways than one. But cease and desist that behavior, and it's possible to restore that child's sense of safety. Resort to repeat physical violence, and the harm that's inflicted corrodes the likelihood of getting that Little One back to safety.

Hurt is a part of everyday relationships, the resulting friction of humans colliding rather than connecting. It's impactful, and we need recovery from it, but the point is that we *can* recover, if it's hurt. Harm suggests an intentional breach of safety, trust, or care.

It's harder to find our way back to safety from harm. Some people never do.

Conversely, if the issue is hurt, not harm, forgiveness can be an empowering antidote to someone else's nonsense. Whatever hurt you're holding, even if someone else gave it to you, it's yours now. You decide what to do with it and what it means for your life.

With this in mind, is it harm that's ongoing? Are you being subjected to intentional and repeated acts of damage? If you are, can anything be done to move you to safety?

If you've somehow come to this book while in a crisis situation, put it down now and get to the internet as fast as possible. Help is available. Please, search until you find it.

Think about it like this: If you were standing on a beach, and a 50-foot wall of ocean was heading your way, you wouldn't in your right mind be considering how to forgive the tsunami, or nature, or whathaveyou. You'd be getting to safety with a quickness.

Do this for yourself with self-protection and boundaries. Use them to get to safety, then you can return to the work of forgiveness to heal yourself and build a healthier future.

Container. My first go at forgiveness happened inside the container, i just didn't know it. But when i shifted my mind from outright rebellion to skeptical willingness, that was me managing the container's set. When we choose to get off the drama triangle - e.g. to own our responsibility and stop villainizing others or forgoing our own power - that's us managing set.

As you make your way toward and through forgiveness, notice and note (like, on your phone's notes app, or in a journal) how your mind is shifting, how your frequency is changing. This is your set, and it will determine the quality of your forgiveness journey.

For setting, i highly recommend identifying at least one person with enough emotional maturity to effectively support you. Like i did unknowingly with 12-step and purposely with my divorce sherpa, put yourself in an environment that can hold your forgiveness efforts safely and sanely. Forgiveness is not a solo venture. Allow at least one other person to be with and shepherd you along the way.

For intention, i say keep it simple: *I intend to be free of whomever and whatever I'm holding as unforgivable. I intend to release myself with forgiveness.* With this intention as your North Star, you will get where you're going on this journey.

For integration, the more support you give yourself, the more effective forgiveness will be for you. Whether it's a professional in behavior change, like a therapist, counselor, or coach, or a wise elder or community group, find someone you trust to share your experience and guide you on how to make it meaningful in your everyday life.

If you can't see how to integrate because you don't have ready access to resources, i suggest you don't stress. Focus on set, setting and intention. Integration opportunities will likely arise organically from people already involved in other parts of your container.

Ultimately, integration flows when we're supported and open to what unfolds naturally.

Prayer. Yeah, i know, this one is like, ugh, seriously?! But this is where you own and exercise your power over the chemistry of how someone or a situation lives inside you.

You don't need to be religious. You don't need to believe in God or a Higher Power. You only need to decide that you're willing to constructively focus your energy and attention on a positive declaration of well-being.

Prayer can be particularly useful if you're of the mind that your healing must or should involve another's acknowledgment and amends for harm caused. The challenge with an amends requirement is it keeps you on the drama triangle. The wrongdoer remains your villain, and you're stuck in the victim role, with power over your healing still in the hands of someone who likely can't stop harming.

As a tool, prayer pries that power out of other people's hands. Directing your energy toward a life force that's bigger than the both of you redirects the current from control to surrender. Surrender opens a pathway to release. Release deactivates our triggers.

This is why we pray.

If you can get your prayer into your body, it'll likely work that much more effectively on your brain. Kneel, if you physically can. And if you can't, define what physical surrender looks like for you. Bow your head. Close your eyes. Look up or down. Speak out loud. Look in the mirror as you say your words. Do what you know you're resistant to doing, and your body will move into the surrender zone and deepen your change.

What you pray for is also for you to decide.

Remember, *you* specifically don't need to forgive to pray for someone's forgiveness. You can pray they be forgiven by whatever is Out There. You can pray to feel neutral. You can pray to stop wanting others to suffer. You can pray for a greater ability to care for yourself, to let go of wanting the sources of harm and hurt to solve your pain.

Decide your prayer, write it down if it helps, and use it as a tool just for you.

Practice. Conventional wisdom says it takes 21 days to form a habit, and just 3 days to break it. Dr. Maxwell Maltz, a plastic surgeon, seeded this unproven idea in a book published in 1960. Maltz noticed it took about 21 days for his patients to adjust to their physical changes, an observation that morphed into habit pop psychology.

The 2009 study "How are habits formed: Modelling habit formation in the real world," published in the *European Journal of Social Psychology*, suggests it can take between 18 to 254 days to form a habit. So yeah, the time frame is all over the place, depending on the habit and the person.

A gold nugget beneath the data has to do with "automaticity" - the ability to do a thing and not occupy your mind with required details. The study is of no help in determining how long it might take to make forgiveness a habit. But it does confirm that "repetition of a behaviour in a consistent context" increases the likelihood of automaticity.

In non-PhD terms, automaticity means you don't need to think or feel so much about a thing to do it. You don't have to push uphill inside yourself. To get to automaticity with forgiveness, do yourself a favor: Practice it consistently.

What i know to do is commit and be consistent for 30 days. Mark 'em on a calendar, and don't let a day slip by without doing what you've committed to do e.g. pray, write, check your set, be with your forgiveness intention, talk to someone about forgiveness.

The more you practice, the more you strengthen forgiveness like a muscle. The more muscle memory your build for forgiveness, the more natural it will be for you to forgive.

/ -.. . -.-. .. -.. . /

Forgiveness entered my life as a guardian archangel, unwelcome, formidable, patient, and flexibly able to work with my ugly prayers and reluctant surrender.

In my construction, forgiveness is a realist. It takes me in and says, "Let's do what we can with what we've got. Whoever, whatever, and wherever you are. I'm here for you."

This is the practice of forgiveness i'm passing along, in case the world and its drama tests and taxes your heart. Consider what you're carrying, and how it feels to be you.

You may not want to forgive.

But do you need to forgive?

That's for you to decide.

If Forgiveness Had Your Number

- *When you say "you" in stories, how often are you really talking about yourself? What truths might you be deflecting?*

- *What unanswered questions keep coming up for you about forgiveness? And if forgiveness was looking for you, what part of your life might it be trying to enter?*

- *Consider the forgiveness tools. What boundaries might help you feel safe about exploring forgiveness? If you tried prayer, what might it sound like for you? What would you pray for? If you tried on forgiveness for 30 days, what's just one act you might commit to practicing?*

13. WHEN PEOPLE LEAVE

Divorce is a multitude of deaths.

The vision of your future dies. Promises die. Your identity and benefits as a married person die. The family and life you created dies. Connections tied to the couplehood sever and die.

If my former spouse had died, she would've left everyone who loved her, and i'd have grieved her in community. There would've been a funeral for everyone to mourn and remember her together, and it wouldn't have been weird at all for me to light a candle for her and hold her in my heart for the rest of my life.

But she didn't leave everyone. She only left me.

Having survived the end of a marriage, i get how people going through divorce can lose themselves to madness. After all the self-work, and the couple's work, i was in despair.

Depression demanded to know: "What is the point of trying at life when it could all just go for a toss?" My suicidal ideation poked its head up to check in: "Welp, if there's no point in trying, do we still wanna be here?" My internal system was making itself clear: If we don't make this loss matter, we might not make it at all.

In the shards of my divorce, decades of doing forgiveness crystallized into a playbook.

Boundaries, prayer, and practice shepherded me through the grief of loss, which really is what's always roiled underneath my resentment, righteousness, and resistance - just a riptide of separation, sadness, disappointment, and devastation pulling at my ankles, yanking me underwater, threatening to drown me in trauma.

Once again, it was the container that alchemized trauma into transcendence.

In the thick of it, my prayer and positive declaration was that the dissolution of my marriage would become not a loss i'd be living, or a pain i'd be holding, but rather a story i could tell of resilience: an indomitable ability to transform trauma into healing, and an insistence on thriving no matter what.

It was a prayer for the integration of my divorce into the larger context of my life story.

Holding onto my set, setting and intention for dear life, my prayer eventually found a response. It was the revelation of what i hadn't known about what i needed from the marriage, what childhood pain the adult relationship had served, and what aspect of me had chosen her to begin with.

This marriage between seeming Grown-Ups had really been a relationship between injured Little Ones: hers anxious, mine abandoned. My hero kept her protected until it didn't. Her love kept me nurtured until it was gone.

If i could go back to our first week together with all i know about how painful our last week would be, i'd do the relationship just as we did. Because if i change even one thing, i risk losing everything i learned. The marriage and divorce were rough-cut gems. Intentionally integrating their lessons into my life showed me, once again, how pain can polish into wisdom and growth.

/ --. --- --- -.. -... -.-- . /

By her lived example, my former spouse taught me to be caring and gentle with myself. With her, i became more playful and creative. Loving someone who moved through life at a more ponderous pace expanded the patience my Beloved Momma had wanted to pray into me. And for all the pain of the divorce, the marriage itself healed my heart and reconnected me to a capacity for compassion and unconditional love.

Most importantly, the full arc of this relationship from first text to final goodbye taught me that when people leave - as so many of them have - it's not because i'm unlovable.

It's because those people just can't stay.

For all that went down with my former spouse, i know she loved me as best she could. The death of our marriage pulled me into a deep, primal grief encoded from inception. Working through the loss delivered a game-changing reframe: i had not now, nor had i ever been, abandoned by someone who didn't love me; i'd been released by someone who could not hold on to me. The nurturing i'd craved all my life, i finally found within myself and for myself once my grief got the message: Love yourself and remember, when people leave, it's because they're unwilling or unable to figure out how to stay.

Integration showed me why i needed not just the marriage, but also, the divorce. It was the leaving that finally stitched together the tear in my heart that began with my birth.

Note to Self, Note to Them

- *Some leavings rewire us, shake our sense of safety, shift how we trust others and ourselves. When life's unraveling and rewiring me, all i can manage at times is a slow walk with no goal, let my heart catch up to my body. What about you?*

- *Maybe you're also thinking of the people who've left you. The ache of that. The patterns of it. The strength it took to survive every single time. You still have you. You still have your brave heart beating in your chest. You still have your breath. Inhale, hold, exhale. You're still here. Isn't that worth noting for yourself?*

- *Maybe you're the one who leaves, the one who can't stay. What's the voice in you that says "go"? What does it cost to follow that voice? If there's a version of goodbye you wish you could give – an honest one, an angry one, a kind one, an unspoken one – can you leave it here?*

14. CHOSEN FAMILY

Once in my late teens just before i left for the military, i'd gotten into a fender-bender on a main street in town. Standing outside my car with the police, my big '80s hair blowing in the wind, i saw my Father drive by. Our eyes met, and i felt him as the last person i needed or wanted to see. We turned away from each other as he drove on.

Forgiving this stranger was an act of self-preservation. It didn't need to involve him.

Forgiving him as my childhood sexual abuser who was my biological Father and with whom i was exploring reconciliation - that got a lot more conditional. Prayer alone couldn't suffice. This situation required confirmation that i was safe, and he'd changed.

He never acknowledged or apologized for who he had been, and i knew he couldn't. Unlike my Mother, who was consumed by the past (but also, never apologized), my Dad limited his reflections to a familiar collection of stories he could comfortably tell.

Several years of sifting through my own trauma made me realize, i had no idea what he'd experienced as a boy. Outside of how much he adored his momma, memorized his multiplication tables by rote from a book, and rocked classic Chuck Taylors as his first pair of cool sneakers, he didn't talk about what it was like for him growing up.

He didn't revisit his own childhood with me, and he didn't revisit mine.

Through family lore, i'd heard my Dad's father kept another woman across town with whom he was having children, all while still married and also having children with my Dad's mother. When my Dad's father died, all manner of relations came to the funeral, which set tongues to wagging. Since i was a just little kid, i didn't know much about it.

What stayed with me was how icky it felt to see his father's dead body in the casket.

After my Parents introduced me to their community for the first time, and i saw how many kids, from toddlers to teens, loved them as surrogate Grandparents, i wrote my Dad a letter. In tempered but no uncertain terms, i told him that i was still healing from his sexual violation of me, that i was counting on him to be responsible and careful with the kids in his life, and that if i ever heard otherwise, i'd personally get involved.

He never mentioned this letter; i had no idea whether he'd received it, read it, and/or shared it with his wife. Their marriage was their business, i didn't know how much he revealed to her. But at least, i had put him on notice.

After my Parents died, i spent 31 days clearing their home of personal items to get it ready for as-is sale to a cousin. On the last day, in the last drawer i cleared, under a stack of unused notepads and ancient paystubs, i found that letter. It'd been opened, and it'd been saved. That was the most i'd ever know about it.

At any moment, i was ready to emotionally sever from him. He never gave me a reason to do so. He just kept being different, and at some point, the change settled in with me.

When i needed respite from the heaviness of my Mother's dying, death and funeral, i called my Dad. Well, actually, i called my Stepmomma, but without my Dad, i wouldn't have had her to call. If she was the light, he was the candle anchoring the flame.

His work ethic and commitment ensured they were stable and reliable - words that had never fit him before. One of the most phenomenal differences between the Father in my childhood and the Dad in my adulthood: His whereabouts were always known to those of us he loved. Anytime he was needed, he was always easy to reach.

He also made a point to call people he cared for. He was insistent about connection.

The second of my 4 university degrees i finished in 2002 at the University of London's School of Oriental and African Studies. My days were long with classes, study groups, research, writing, and 90-minute commutes to and from school.

So, yeah, it wasn't awesome when the "in case of an emergency" landline phone in my flat trilled me awake at roughly 3 o'clock in the morning my time.

"Whatcha doin?" said the now-familiar Papa Bear voice on the other end.

"Umm, I'm sleeping. It's the middle of the night here. Everything alright?"

"Yeah, everything's alright. How's the weather over there? Is it rainin'?"

"Uh, I don't know how the weather is because it's dark, and I'm sleeping."

"Huh. Whatchu eat today?"

"I had some Indian food, it's really good over here."

"Huh. Well, I hadn't heard your voice in a while. I just called to hear your voice."

"Oh, OK Dad, thanks. Lemme call you back soon, when i'm awake."

"OK, love you, Babygirl."

"Love you, too, Dad."

It had been 4 years since the Balcony Reveal. With forgiveness, not only could i say it, i could actually mean it: i loved him, and he was my Dad.

/ -.-. .... --- ... . -. /

Finding the woman who'd given birth to me had never been on my list of things to do.

My life was already littered with parental fails, and i didn't imagine a movie-magical reunion. You know that saying, "You only get one Mother"? Not so if you're adopted. As many adults as it took for me to get functional parents, clearly, i should be done.

Also, my Stepmomma - my Beloved Momma - unilaterally assigned responsibility to me for seeing after her transition. "I saw how you did with your Mother. You're the one, you're gonna be takin' care of me," she straight-up volun-told me. She was a daughter who had looked after her mother. Now she had a daughter who would look after her.

"Of course I'ma take care of you," i promised her. "I was there for my Mother because she raised me. I'ma be there for you because you love me." But there was one caveat.

"You ain't gon' like it, but you're gonna have in-home care. I'm not doing it by myself." Averse to the idea of strangers in her home, she said we'd see about it down the road.

This is why i was no longer accepting applications for parents. The last thing i needed were more people to process about now, or ferry and bury later.

Also, i didn't feel a need to find her because i didn't feel i needed anything from her. Not reconciliation, not repair, not anything. Though i'd been told she was my "real" mother, to me, she was words on parched official papers. She didn't feel real at all.

But a series of you-can't-make-this-stuff-up serendipities brought her into my life because, apparently, the plot needed a kaleidoscopic twist.

The London school i attended boasted a diverse student body repping 150+ countries. One of my classmates happened to be a German woman from a village near Stuttgart, where i was born and adopted. She offered to introduce me to my birth city as a native tour guide and translator, as i didn't speak a decent word of German.

She also said, if i was curious about my birth mother, she'd help me find the law office where it all started. We set off on the adventure, found the law office, learned the legal advisor who'd handled my adoption had passed away, and were told that their official records of my adoption were sealed until the end of time.

It was summer 2002, an even year. Europeans, you know what that means. Football (soccer, Americans) blared from every TV in every restaurant, café, and bar in the city.

Waiters at the Italian spot we stopped into for lunch were shouting at their TV. Italy was down 1-nil to Mexico. We arrived before a late equalizer saved the match with a tie.

Before joining their watch party, i just did not understand running up and down a field for nearly 2 hours, only to have the whole thing end in a tie. Growing up on American football indoctrinated me to root for winners. By the end of the watch-party, the grace and shared excitement of the world's Beautiful Game had baptized me into fandom.

Nothing more would've come out of Stuttgart if my classmate and i hadn't started dating. Fast-friendship swiftly ignited a relationship that enticed me to Berlin, where i studied German in the mornings and taught English in the afternoons.

Before i could string together a coherent sentence in German, i learned *Geburtsmutter* from an exacting German social worker who helped me through the process of signing up for the free German healthcare to which i was entitled. But how had i landed in his office in my 30s with a German passport and no German language skills, he wondered.

Rifling through 400 pages of the dense German dictionary i carried everywhere in the pre-smartphone early-aughts, my garbled explanation of a German 19-year-old and an American soldier making a baby she couldn't keep led to *Geburtsmutter*, birth mother.

That day, a random bespectacled middle-aged German man whose name i never knew helped me cracked the code of my conception. *Geburtsmutter* gave me new language and logic to define and describe my beginnings.

She wasn't my "real" mother. She was my Birth Mother. THAT was real.

Now i could factually label her, but i still didn't know who or where she was, and i still wasn't all that interested in looking.

Then the German woman i was dating got word her mother, who'd lived for decades with cancer, had been admitted to the hospital near her home village. The hamlet of 300 residents was probably similar to where my Father had met my Birth Mother.

Weekend plans to visit and help her temporarily relocate morphed into nearly a year of living in her family home in the Black Forest after her Mom passed away. My teaching job in Berlin transferred to Stuttgart, and i spent nearly every weekday commuting to the city where i had arrived into the world.

English language instruction is not a lucrative financial endeavour for most teachers. In need of a career boost after a year, i signed on for my third university degree, an MBA, and made plans to head back to the U.S. in 2004

The question arose of whether to look for my Birth Mother once more before leaving Stuttgart for good. Half-heartedly, i looked online for the address to social services and discovered i'd spent every weekday for the better part of a year working 4 blocks down the street from the Stuttgart social services bureau that housed child welfare records.

My final day of teaching work was on a Friday, and i'd lived in Germany long enough to know a few things about the country's public servants: they don't work for several days around Christmas and Easter; they don't work for at least a month during summer; and they don't work after 3pm on Fridays.

A part of me wanted nothing to do with this quest, but my relentless curiosity would not accept being so close and not exploring further. In an act of self-sabotage, i set out for the social services office at 2:45pm. The building's lobby was empty when i arrived, save for one security guard, who escorted me up to the child welfare department. This floor was also lights-off and cubicles-empty, save for one person filing paperwork.

Pulling out my German dictionary, i put forth my inquiry. She sat me down in an office, stepped out, and returned in a few minutes with a green file folder. A half-inch thick, it bore the name that my Birth Mother had given me, according to my birth certificate.

As casually as a waiter hands a menu to a guest, she handed my origin story to me. It was like i was entitled to it, and she'd simply been holding onto it, awaiting my arrival.

The first thing i noticed when i opened the file were signatures on a document from the people identified as parents. Each signature was listed beneath a signee statement that confirmed they were the parent, and they were relinquishing all rights to the child.

The mother's signature section showed a name i recognized.

The father's signature section featured a name i didn't expect.

It was not my Father.

To be sure i was reading correctly, i asked the person helping me, "This is the father? Are we sure this is the father?" She looked perplexed, like, why else would a man go through the trouble of signing a form releasing parental rights if he wasn't the father.

But if this man was the father, then who is the man who thinks he's my Father?

The person assisting me said she'd search databases for my Birth Mother and contact me if more info became available. She couldn't help locate my Birth Father, she said, because he wasn't a German citizen at my birth, so there wouldn't be identity records.

She walked me to a copy machine, scanned every document in the half-inch-thick file, handed me the originals in their green folder, and wished me *Schönes Wochenende!*

My "nice weekend" began with a 15-hour flight from Stuttgart to California, where i now had yet another parental puzzle to solve.

/ -.-. .... --- ... . -. /

Two weeks later and bored to tears in a Macroeconomics class, i checked my email to find a message from German social services. My Birth Mother had been found. She'd agreed i could contact her. They listed her address and phone number, and wished me *eine schöne Woche.*

My Birth Mother had been found. She wanted to hear from me.

Whether i was having a "good week" i couldn't yet say – i didn't know how to feel.

It didn't seem right to make either of us wait for a call we both knew was coming, so i got on with it. Two highlights stayed with me from our first long-distance conversation.

The sound of her voice landed like hard living. It was rough, low, and scratchy. It was the voice of a chain-smoker. It wasn't pleasant to listen to her, and that felt kind of sad.

The other highlight was her answer to the question: Who is my father?

She told me he was a Black student from Biafra, a self-declared independent republic in West Africa. His family sent him to Europe to study conveniently during Biafra's civil war with Nigeria from 1967 to 1970. She met him in Stuttgart, she said. It was a fling. They hadn't intended anything more. She was pregnant when they signed the papers giving me to the government. They parted ways, and she never saw him again.

Her recounting would've been perfectly believable and unquestioned, if i didn't already have a biological father who recalled part of her name.

Her parents bestowed Victorian-era multi-syllabic first and middle names on a child conceived in a Leipzig refugee camp for *Volksdeutsche*. These were ethnic Germans expelled from Eastern Europe during World War II. Her parents' German descendants had been rooted in Romania for generations. War undid their lives and their lineage in the blink of an eye. Their ornately named child carried their nostalgia in her identity.

This, of course, wasn't how she eventually described her family's woeful history to me. She had primary school English language skills – clunky grammar and a rudimentary vocabulary. But she could nonetheless express her essentials and convey her story.

Had she ever met a man with my Father's name, i asked in that first call. She said no, she hadn't known a man by that name. Is it possible she knew him, i pressed. He was an American soldier. He says he is my father, and he knew a woman with her name.

She still used her middle name, not her first name, as her everyday name. This is the name my Father recalled. But no, she insisted, she didn't know him. The only man she knew was a student from Africa, and he was my father.

For 3 years, we communicated by phone and postal mail. She didn't own a computer.

She wrote her letters in German, and i used my dictionary to get through them. She said she'd expected i'd find her, that sometimes, she'd look out of her window for me. She wondered what i looked like growing up. She asked if i'd had a good childhood.

She sent me a photo of her at 19, long-haired with a long oval face, wide eyes, sharp nose, and a thin mouth. We literally looked nothing alike.

Subsequent photos showed her hair buzzed close to her head, her ears sticking out from the sides. She dressed unstylishly in plain slacks and single-colored sweaters or loose-fitting dresses covering her thin legs. She wore little or no make-up, stood stiffly, and squinted unsmilingly at the camera. A few photos showed a cigarette delicately held between the fingertips of her index and middle fingers.

Aside from a shared lack of fashion sense, i saw none of me in her.

In subsequent conversations, i confirmed that she had indeed used the same legal office to give me up for adoption that my Father had used to adopt me. If i mentioned his name, she'd consistently reiterate, she didn't know who he was.

She said her family refused to let her keep a mixed-race baby, and she had no means to keep me on her own. She could visit me in the orphanage after i was born, she said, so she spent her afternoons there, holding me. No one told her i'd been adopted. One afternoon, she arrived, and i was gone.

Her letters and voice didn't convey much emotion, but she wasn't cold. She shared her difficult details with the stoicism of a realist, and welcomed an opportunity to meet me.

/ -.-. .... --- ... . -. /

A few weeks after the first conversation with my Birth Mother, i was on the phone with my Dad. Per usual, we covered the weather and what i'd eaten. To maneuver us from the mundane to the more serious topic on my mind, i told him that i was thinking about going back to Germany once i graduated with my MBA.

"Oh yeah?" He talked about wanting to travel to Germany with my Beloved Momma, but that wasn't gonna happen because she had a debilitating fear of flying.

"I'd like to travel there with you, Dad, maybe visit Stuttgart, where I was born?"

"Yeah, that'd be alright."

"Dad, I was thinking, did you get to see me after I was born?"

"Whatchu mean?"

"Well, I went into an orphanage, right? Did you get to see me there?"

“Naw, I couldn’t see you until we finished the adoption. It took a few months.”

“Huh. The German woman, did you ever see her again?”

“Not after she told me about you.”

“Hmm. Dad, you think there’s a chance she mighta been seeing someone else when you knew her?”

“I mean, she coulda, but I didn’t know nothing about it.”

“What I’m wondering is, how did you know I was yours?

“Whatchu mean?”

“I mean, she told you. But, if there was a chance I wasn’t yours . . .?”

My Dad cut me off. “I don’t wanna know no shit like that.”

And he never did, not explicitly, not from me.

/ -.-. .... --- ... . -. /

My Birth Mother and i met in 2006, after i finished my MBA and could visit the village in southern Germany where she lived with a husband. Like her slacks and sweaters, their home was modest and plain, a 2-bedroom duplex neatly kept without art or decor.

She hosted me for 3 days.

On Day 1, she told me about her family. She didn’t seem to be close to them, and she didn’t suggest i meet anyone else. She had no other children, just her marriage.

On Day 2, she told me that after she gave me up, she had a love affair with a woman who broke her heart. But in any case, she realized she hadn’t been made for a man. Her marriage was one of convenience to a dandy who, in his 70s, was still in the closet.

On Day 3, she handed me an envelope with 3,000 Euro. In anticipation of seeing me again, she said, it was as much as she'd been able to save over her lifetime.

In person, she felt fragile. She didn't cry, but her hands shook when she held mine. She touched my arms, my face, my hair. She sat hip-to-hip for photos. One photo captured her gazing at me, thin lips curved in a half-smile. Her emotion was subtle, but palpable.

Sitting at her 2-seat kitchen table with cups of weak tea and my German dictionary, she asked, with earnest concern, questions i'd not yet answered: Were my parents good parents? Did i have a good childhood?

Only because she's no longer around to read this, i can say that, at the time, i flat-out lied. "Sure," i said, a word i employed to ready myself to tell the lie i was about to tell.

"Sure, it was a good childhood. Everything turned out good."

Mercifully, she asked no follow-up questions, and we moved on.

From back when i was 9, i already knew, the parents i had couldn't always handle the truth. As someone who prefers to learn hard lessons once, i allowed my Birth Mother's existence in my life to kick off a whole new era of lying to parents.

When a woman reconnecting with a child she gave up 30+ years ago asks whether that child had a good childhood, she needs the truth to be yes. She needs to believe her years of guilt and remorse were worth it. She needs to believe she did the right thing.

Who was i to say she didn't?

It took a bunch of reps, but i got Parents who loved me and whom i get to love forever.

No, i didn't know at the time how it would all turn out. So yeah, maybe factually, i lied. But, who knows, maybe my lie was a prayer, a positive declaration to the Universe that everything would be OK in the end.

As far as i'm concerned, all's well that ends well. Best that she be none the wiser.

Same with my Dad.

The Old Soldier caught a case of the fragiles about my well-being in adulthood that'd been missing entirely in my childhood. Like when he had an actual mini-stroke from worry after i had hip surgery in my 40s. Sometimes, he just needed to not know stuff.

What i didn't want him to know, i didn't share with his wife: i didn't tell my Parents about finding the lump in my throat; i didn't tell them about finding my Birth Mother.

He didn't need to know that a DNA test confirmed she'd given birth to me. He didn't need to know that, according to her, he wasn't my father.

/ -.-. .... --- ... . -. /

In 2007, on a typical and regular day, my Birth Mother called to announce that she was cutting all contact with me. Like a company downsizing its staff, she was letting me go.

If you're thinking "WTF?!" – multiply that vibe by infinity, and you're somewhere near how violently and outrageously abrupt it felt, how completely out-of-the-effin-blue.

The center of my chest tore open. A fiery assortment of expletives flew out.

Why the _______ would she do this now? We were 3 years in. We talked a couple times a month with no discernible friction. What the _______ was going on?

My Father was not my father, she said, and she couldn't be OK with him in my life. In her mind, it was unacceptable that i would hold my Father's truth as equal to her own.

In my mind, that was the stupidest effing excuse. My Father had nothing to do with her. He didn't even know she was alive or in my life. What kind of effed up reason was this?

How could she do this? What the _______ was WRONG with her?

My rhetorical questions were provocations with painful answers shaped by shock.

She's forsaking me.

She doesn't want me.

She only cares about her.

She doesn't care about me.

She's turning her back on me.

My conclusions were the primal wailing cries of a helpless infant thrashing in my body, severed from its mother, and colicky with abandonment.

Now i could see it was the infant part of me that wanted nothing to do with finding her. The cord that was supposed to bind us for life had been cut. The loss preceded word and memory. It lived in my infant body. This part of me knew she'd given me up once.

This part of me also knew that she could let me go again before i even realized i'd been holding on to her.

Es tut mir sehr leid, she told me, before she hung up the phone.

Loosely translated, she said "I'm very sorry."

Literally translated, she said: "It does me much pain. It causes me much sorrow."

Why would she do more pain? Why would she cause more sorrow?

In the intensity of the moment, my anguished questions weren't reaching for insights.

Then, that same week, Dad delivered knee-buckling news of my Beloved Momma's heart attack. The close call colored my grief and loss with gratitude and love. It didn't erase the pain, but softened its edges, making room in me for reflection and revelation.

/ -.-. .... --- ... . -. /

As a kid, i'd held no anger for my Birth Mother. It didn't matter if she didn't want me. She gave me exactly what i needed to survive my childhood: She made me different.

A long-ago friend once told me that people are driven by 1 of 3 imperatives: to be first, to be the best, or to be different. Because of her, i had an imperative that worked like a super-power. It gave me a clear-eyed ability to see the brokenness around me. It gave me the emotional fortitude i needed to separate and protect myself from my childhood parents. It gave me the determination to shift my trajectory and heal myself.

Difference was the super-power i used to grind intergenerational trauma to a halt.

In early adulthood, there'd been no need to forgive a severance that felt circumstantial. At 19, she got pregnant. At 19, i came out and attempted to kill myself. For both of us, 19 was an age of desperate decisions. It wasn't hard to have a heart for her situation.

The second severance felt personal.

She'd seen me, reached for connection, then pulled away. This woman, who'd been neither present nor a presence for most of my life, was now a real pain point. If i didn't attend to this, she could become a festering resentment. Once again, i leaned on my go-to practice for parental clean-up.

Forgiveness eased me back from injury and walked me around to her side of the pain. Once i could see her trauma monster, i just could not hold it against her.

Nothing about her indicated that she found a healthy or happy way forward. She was sad, resigned, and stuck. She didn't want an adult child. She wanted her baby back.

She'd held onto me every day that she could. My Father took me away from her, and now i loved him. She'd lost me to him once. She couldn't risk losing me to him again. Her trauma monster didn't know how to find safety in connection. It convinced her to let me go. At least now she could stop looking out her window for me. She could know that i'm OK, and maybe find a little peace.

Like my Mother, my Birth Mother had an opportunity to heal, but her trauma monster wouldn't allow it. Reconnection didn't work for her. Turns out, separation didn't either.

In 2019, she dialed my number, which hadn't changed since 2007. Her husband had died. She was alone. She was going blind. She asked me to call, and visit if i wanted.

When i said sure, i'd do that, i honestly didn't intend to lie.

But her chapter had closed in me, and it would not be reopened. My acceptance of her was not approval. My forgiveness for her was not excusal.

On the way to forgiving her, i needed also to forgive myself for pushing past the inner wisdom of my infant body. The warning about her was there. Because i didn't know how to address it, i ignored it. There's no regret, rather a lesson: If my body talks, listen.

The serendipities that brought me to my Birth Mother were looking for connections to nurture and nourish me. They were looking for family. Her choice to separate solidified what family means for me. She birthed and named me, but she would never be family.

Family is more than a name for me. It's who we claim. It's more than who we're given. It's who chooses us, and who we choose.

In my origin story's motley cast of characters, my Father is the only one who chose me.

The man made a mess of my childhood, but he did one thing right. He chose me. Then, i chose him. Together, our choices made us family and changed our lives for the better.

/ -.-. .... --- ... . -. /

My oldest and dearest friend is on her cellphone with me in the final days of a business venture she's decided to shut down. Something to do with drug testing for commercial drivers. Her office phone rings, and she takes the call.

Yes, she says, they do paternity testing. Yes, she says, you can do it through the mail.

"Are you serious?!" i say incredulously, once we're back on the phone. She's one of few people in my life who know there's a possibility my Dad isn't my biological father.

"All this time, i've had access to a paternity test with someone i trust?! Could you do this for me?" She tells me as long as my Dad consents to a DNA sample, she'll take care of the test and rush the results.

My Dad has his truth. He doesn't want any more facts. When i tell him i need his saliva for health-related DNA testing, he asks me no questions, and i tell him no further lies.

It's 2019, i know who my family is, i know what's true, but i still don't know what's real.

The legal advisor has passed away. There's no one alive who can tell me what really happened the day i left the orphanage. Why did i go to the man who claimed me? Was it a baby-swap? Was the swap accidental? Or maybe intentional? Did another baby's mother change her mind and keep her child? But i was still available, so i subbed in?

Or, and this was hard, but i questioned, did my Birth Mother actually know my Father, but he'd done something bad? Had he violated her, and she didn't want me to know?

If my Dad was my father from birth, i'd know he hadn't been bamboozled, but i'd have painful questions ahead. If my Dad was not my father from birth, i'd never tell him. And, i'd need to make sense of a life story that technically wasn't even supposed to happen.

The DNA test wouldn't fill in the blanks, but it would narrow the possibilities, and that would have to suffice. The results arrived, and i drove them to therapy unopened.

My therapist's office was a safe cocoon. It held everything i brought. It was a place where my worst experiences became gateways to freedom. We transformed trauma into gifts and integrated those gifts into my life. What would we alchemize next?

My therapist opened, absorbed, and read me the results: My Dad was not my father.

/ -.-. .... --- ... . -. /

"Yo Sis! I gotta tell you about your Pops last night, call me back!" It's a close family friend, 10 years younger than me, whom i babysat when we were kids. Our fathers were Army brothers, and he loves my Dad like he loves his own Dad.

He's staying with my Dad for several weeks following my Beloved Momma's death.

The urgency in his message prompts me to ring him back right away. He tells me that he awoke the night before to a noise he didn't recognize. It sounded, he says, like an animal in pain. It was my Dad. Opening the door to my Dad's bedroom, he found him standing in front of the mirror, naked from the waist down. He was crying, delirious.

The friend asked, "What's going, on Pops? What's happening? What's wrong whichu?"

My Dad didn't answer directly. Instead, he looked in the mirror and started shouting "Touch it!" repeatedly. Then he backed himself away from the mirror into a corner, folding his oversized-bear frame onto the floor with his knees drawn to his chest.

The family friend just so happened to be trained in emergency response and crisis de-escalation. No one i can think of was better positioned to be in this moment with my Dad and eventually talk and guide him back into bed for the night.

"Whaddyou think it's about?" he asks me. What i think, i don't say. It stays with me as a revelation. It takes me back to that question i asked rhetorically on the balcony with my Dad many years ago: "What kind of a human being violates their own child?"

My Dad's lucid delirium suggests the obvious answer: Someone who'd been sexually violated as a child. It's not a rocket science revelation, but it's powerful. It reminds me that what i don't know about my Dad far exceeds what i do.

All that i've lived, seen, and endured with my many parents has, over time, unraveled the impulse to reduce them to criticisms like cruel, crazy, vile, and deliberately harmful.

They may've been all of those things, but more than anything, they were traumatized.

Their damage and wounds were energies, jagged forces that moved through them and into me. Physics tells us that energy isn't destroyed, only transferred and transformed. My parental relationships ran on a kind of emotional physics, and perhaps that was our purpose together: They transferred their trauma to me, and i transformed it into healing.

/ -.-. .... --- ... . -. /

There are 2 hopes i have for this book: that it inspires you to free yourself from your Unforgivables, and that no one who knows and loves my Dad ever reads it – i don't want the person he was to ruin the person he became.

While i can't recall what i said to my Dad after his balcony revelation, revisiting and reliving the moment brings me to tears: i wish there'd been more healing between us then; i wish that i could've said to him then what i can imagine saying to him now.

Standing in front of my Father, i open my arms. One of my hands holds the center of my own chest. My other hand, i rest on his chest, like i'll do with my Beloved Momma when she takes her last breath.

"Thank you," i tell him, "for choosing me. What you did, it was brave. It was honorable. It was selfless, protective, and strong. It was everything that defines a Dad. I'm grateful you're willing to change. I'm proud of who you're becoming. I'm OK to be like you."

A few days after my Dad died, my therapist said to me during our session, "You are gonna be in a relationship with your Dad for the rest of your life. The amazing thing is, it's all up to you now, you get to completely choose what the relationship looks like."

Because i've forgiven him, and because i can, i choose to love him.

If anyone who knows and loves my Dad reads this book - i'm hoping you don't, but if you do - and you're betrayed or pained by what you've read, i ask, please, forgive him.

I have. I hope you can, too.

Not for me. Not for him.

Forgive for you.

Family, Forgiveness & Freedom

- *What does "family" mean to you – is it blood, choice, tribe? The people in your life today whom you call family, what makes them family to you? What makes you family to them?*

- *Sometimes, waiting on some folks to acknowledge and apologize for harm be like waiting until we're taller (or shorter) to be happy with our height. We're held hostage to circumstances that just aren't gonna change. But you already know my take. What's your take on forgiving someone who will never say sorry?*

- *What do you think, if you've been deeply hurt, is it possible to *not* forgive and still feel yourself free of hurt and resentment? And, if you are holding a hurt that someone's given you, what would it mean to forgive, not for them, for you?*

Postface

Not until i finished *Forgive For You* did it hit me: i spent roughly 5,000 hours writing a book about unconditional forgiveness.

It's an outrageous notion in a world where we typically reserve our unconditional best for kids, pets, or a trusted few. But what's the alternative? Stay mired in our divisions, grudges, and feuds? That's not safe. It's sorrowful. It's a state that's ripe for disruption.

If something in these pages calls to you, carry it forward, not as a burden, as a prompt. Up against our challenges, the outrageousness of unconditional forgiveness dares us to be more. It's a living, breathing charge to choose peace, even when it's outrageous, especially when it's outrageous. Long before i had a label for this, i lived the proof of it.

Looking back after 5,000 hours with *Forgive For You*, it feels to me now like i've been writing this book since the day i was born.

To the people who gave me these stories, wherever you may be, i hope you're all OK.

To friends and supporters who listened to me lament and thrash my way through this process, our conversations were not for naught. Stick a fork in this thing – it's done!

To the crews at Manuscripts and the Manhattan Book Group who helped shape my life into a publishable product despite me, thank you for being patiently good at your jobs.

To Dalveer, who gave me safe haven to write and survive amidst terrifying uncertainty, hey, Girl, heeyyyy!

To Cameron, Emily, Glodean, Jennie, Kathy, Kay, Maija, Rachel, Reid, Sia – this book isn't fit for print without your thoughtful insights and push. Unending thanks to you all.

To anyone who reads this, i sincerely appreciate you spending time with me, for you.

We are not alone, and we do not heal alone. We heal in the company of truth, courage, and chosen kin. May we find all three, again and again and again.

– luca

Author's Bio

Luca Oake is the Founder and Chief Forgiveness Officer of YFFY | You Forgive For You, the safest, sanest place on the internet to explore and practice forgiveness.

YFFY is pronounced yiffy, it sounds like jiffy, and it's a movement to make forgiveness a practical, learnable skill for well-being, longevity, resilience, and high performance.

Professionally, Luca is an advisor, author, and avid learner with 4 university degrees, decades of experience in adult development, and an irrational passion for forgiveness.

Personally, Luca is a neurodivergent, nonbinary, cis-gender-nonconforming woman. Though frequently and erroneously referred to as "sir" in person and over the phone, Luca's preferred pronoun is *oui*. But *she* or *they* will also do.

To say Luca's last name correctly, just think "oak" like the tree.

Luca wrote this book with the lyrics of a favorite Prince song in mind:

All of this
and more
is for you

With love,
sincerity,
and deepest care,

my life
with you
i share

For more about Luca, start here:
linkedin.com/in/heylucaoake

For a safe place to practice forgiveness, start here:
youforgiveforyou.community

www.ingramcontent.com/pod-product-compliance
Lightning Source LLC
LaVergne TN
LVHW052352100826
845147LV00013B/818

9798986587349